THE MARTYR'S CROWN

THE MARTYR'S CROWN

Rome and the English Church

PAUL KEANE

FAMILY PUBLICATIONS

© 2009 Family Publications, Oxford

Images © Venerabile Collegio Inglese

Photographs by Fabio Ravà

ISBN 978 1 907380 00 6

published by
Family Publications
Denis Riches House, 66 Sandford Lane
Oxford OX1 5RP
www.familypublications.co.uk

Printed in Malta
through s|s|media ltd

Contents

Acknowledgments

I am indebted to: Rev'd Mgr Tony Philpot for his translation of the wall paintings' Latin annotations; Rev'd Gerard Flynn – a true son of the brothers of Aruald – and the Parish of St Saviour's, Totland Bay, for their very generous hospitality; Rev'd Dr Stewart Foster, Rev'd Dr David Forrester, Rev'd Dr Adrian Graffy, Lorna Harper, Sr Mary Joseph McManamon OSB and Lucy Qureshi for reading different parts of the text and their helpful suggestions and corrections; Rev'd Gerard Skinner for his advice and allowing a change to holiday plans; the Librarian of Ampleforth Abbey, the Parish of the Cathedral of SS. Mary and Helen, Brentwood, Rev'd Andrew Headon, Rev'd Dominic Howarth, Rev'd Mgr Nicholas Hudson, Geraldine Kilkelly, The London Library, Rev'd Jean-Laurent Marie, Rev'd Mgr William Nix, Rev'd Nicholas Schofield, and Joel's Bar, for their assistance.

'A Powerful Place'

I took a young French woman to see the Tribune; and when we had seen half the frescoes, she stopped me to say, 'It's a powerful place!', 'C'est un lieu fort, tu sais!' She was referring not only to the Tribune but to the whole College.

A former student, recalling his arrival at the College, said to me recently, 'Didn't you feel, when you were first shown those frescoes, that you were becoming part of an extraordinarily rich tradition?' I believe he spoke for four centuries of students – who have looked up at these images and wondered if they would have had a fraction of the courage of these their forebears.

It is said that students in the College's first decades used to contemplate these frescoes as one would contemplate Stations of the Cross – only they recognised in the pictures the faces of priests with whom they had lived on this site.

It is a powerful place. And Fr Paul Keane has captured its strength extraordinarily well. His book puts these images truly in context but will also serve to deepen their devotional power. I thank him and salute him for this achievement.

Mgr Nicholas Hudson
Rector, Venerable English College, Rome

Introduction

Via di Monserrato is close to the River Tiber in the historical centre of Rome. It is a narrow, winding street with tall *palazzi,* leaving above you only a ribbon of sky. Its name comes from one of its churches, Santa Maria di Monserrato, dedicated to the great shrine of the Black Madonna of Montserrat. Above its door is a sculpture of Mary steadying the Christ child as he holds a saw and cuts away into rock – Montserrat means 'serrated mountain'. Within the church are the remains of the Borgia pope, Alexander VI, exiled from St Peter's.

Close by is a building taking up almost an entire block, that from the outside is a mixture of *palazzo*, church, cafe and lighting shop. This is the Venerable English College, the oldest British institution outside Britain. Over time the fabric has altered, walls have moved, a church has disappeared and been rebuilt, but the nucleus of this bit of Rome has been British since at least 1362, when a hospice was founded here for English pilgrims. The Reformation made the journey to Rome difficult and new needs appeared. In 1579 the hospice formally became a seminary, founded by Pope Gregory XIII with the encouragement of William Allen. With the other earlier English College at Douai, this place dedicated itself to the training of men for the Catholic priesthood in England and Wales – a ministry which was soon to be banned by English law. Nevertheless, from its earliest days the students swore the missionary oath, promising that on the completion of their studies they would return home, 'come rack, come rope'.

The main entrance of the college brings you into a long, light and high corridor with an enclosed garden at its end. From the right of the corridor, a wide staircase, turning four times, leads you to the *piano nobile* – the principal floor with the finest rooms. There, off a corridor lined with the pictures of English cardinals, is a short, unlit flight of stairs. Push open the door at the top and you will find yourself in a space with many windows, yet which is always somewhat in the dark. It is the tribune, a wide balcony which runs three sides of the college church, two-thirds up the height of the church walls. You will have noticed immediately that the walls of the tribune at eye-level and above are painted with pictures, but as your eyes become more sensitive details appear: a woman in flames; a man being flayed alive; nuns cutting off their own noses; limbs boiling in cauldrons. You could forgive yourself thinking that like Alex in *A Clockwork Orange* you are being subjected to the Ludovico Technique: exposure to scenes of violence to heal you of violence.

These wall paintings, finished in 1583, tell the history of the Catholic Church in England and Wales from a perhaps mythical beginning in the year 63 until events in 1583 itself, some of which had not yet happened when the artist had begun to paint. The focus is the saints of England and Wales but not ones like St David, St Edward the Confessor or St Hugh of Lincoln, who died peacefully in bed. The saints in these paintings were brought to birth in heaven by violence: racked, speared, beheaded. They are England and Wales' martyrs; their torturous deaths are not left to the imagination. In all there are thirty-four separate scenes or pictures, involving, if you exclude eleven thousand martyrs in one, and a few thousand in another, around one hundred and fifty different characters. The pictures are remorselessly gory, yet they tell a true story: the glorious deaths of English and Welsh men and women for the Gospel of Christ and the unity of the Church.

In a way the purpose of the pictures is obvious: a celebration of martyrdom for a college of martyrs. Some of the last scenes include men who, only a few years before, had been students in the college. But the pictures are also a response to a controversy. Since the 1540s, various English reformers and Protestants had been busy. They had attacked traditional heroes and saints; celebrated long-reviled traitors and heretics. They had torn out the historical roots of the English and Welsh Church, long planted deep and often watered by papal effort, to replace them with – if you can replace roots – phantom tales of hidden Churches free of Rome's corruption. To put it plainly: they had rewritten English and Welsh history. These pictures are a Catholic response. As the Jesuit Robert Persons later commented, only by studying planting, continuation and succession in the Church could 'the whole controversy between us and the Protestants fully be cleared.' History had become the battlefield, where, with the witness of the martyrs as their arms and miracles as their shields, Catholics would have to fight for the proof of Catholic continuity. Most importantly, they would have to show that the Church in England and Wales and the Bishop of Rome were providentially and necessarily always linked throughout history.

To understand and appreciate more deeply the wall paintings, this book will consider the arguments and events that led to their creation. Its first chapter will look at the reformers' new understanding of English and Welsh Church history in the writings of John Bale. The next three chapters will chart the Catholic response, led by St Thomas More, Cardinal Reginald Pole and Thomas Stapleton. The fifth to eighth chapters will show how the historical debate between Protestants and Catholics came to be expressed in paint. Finally, we will simply explore and enjoy the wall paintings.

The thirty-four separate pictures are a unique record of England and Wales' past and deserve to be better known. They remind us that, however mistaken either side may have been, both loved their country. Because of that love they fought ferociously, fearing that loss of England and Wales' past would lead to loss of England and Wales' future.

The pictures are graphic. I have known people to feel queasy before them. We should be challenged by acts of violence. Yet to appreciate them appropriately, we must remember that Christians have long celebrated martyrdom: the witness of individuals to the endurance of faith, hope and love. The first saint of the Church – the Good Thief – was born into Heaven from the Cross; the second, St Stephen, by the clatter of stones. Martyrdom should not be sought but when it is the inevitable result of choices made out of love, then it should be celebrated. As an act of love, it is exquisitely beautiful. The great historian, St Bede, saw the beauty of St Alban's martyrdom reflected in its setting. The hill where he was beheaded 'as was fitting . . . was fair, shining and beautiful, adorned, indeed clothed, on all sides with wild flowers of every kind; nowhere was it steep or precipitous or sheer but Nature had provided it with wide, long-sloping sides stretching smoothly down to the level of the plain. In fact its natural beauty had long fitted it as a place to be hallowed by the blood of a blessed martyr.'

Chapter 1

THE MYTHMAKER

The mud cliffs of Suffolk are crumbling, falling away. Covehithe, between Lowestoft and Southwold, had been a busy enough port but over five hundred years ago it was eaten up by the tides and all that now remains are a few houses, St Andrew's church and a road going nowhere. The church tower is magnificent but only part of the walls of the chancel and nave still stand; having lost its monastic patron at the Dissolution of the Monasteries, the church was plundered for building material. It is a beautiful, lonely ruin.

John Bale was born into a humble family in Covehithe on 21 November 1495. We must begin with him because ninety years later the paintings on the English College walls would be a response to his writings and arguments. He is the unwitting grandfather of our story.

When he was eleven years old Bale was sent to study at the Carmelite priory in Norwich. The Order had come to England in 1242 with returning crusaders. Originally a group of hermits, with no single founder but inspired by the example of Elijah, they lived in loose relationship with each other on Mount Carmel. In the early thirteenth century a Rule of Life binding them more closely together was adopted and, forced by Islamic incursions, they moved west. In 1247, Pope Innocent IV approved certain amendments to the Carmelites' Rule that reflected their exile to the business of Western Christendom and they became mendicants and preachers like the Franciscans and Dominicans. Their houses were numerous; at the height of the Order there were at least one thousand Carmelites in England. They acted as confessors to Henry IV and Henry V. They did not produce the most able scholars but in the 1300s they were the prominent critics of the influential and heretical teaching of the Oxford lecturer, John Wyclif. Bale was to be a Carmelite for thirty years, for most of those years a very proud one.

In 1514 he was sent to Cambridge for further studies and remained sixteen years. This was a golden age for the university. The chancellor was the Bishop of Rochester, St John Fisher. He excelled at raising money for new colleges and in support of the latest learning, including the study of Hebrew and Greek. The Carmelite priory was on the Cam just north of Queens' College. It was a great location. It looked away from the bustle of the town but could supply itself with ease from the river. Its buildings were various, including a church with tower and belfry, cloisters, a kitchen block and a dormitory set amidst extensive grounds. Immediately north of the priory, King's College chapel rose in perpendicular splendour. Its fan vaulting was the finest in the land and its windows were being filled with the most gorgeous stained glass. And at Queens', just before Bale arrived, the greatest Humanist scholar, Erasmus, had left, leaving a hunger for more. It was the young Carmelite's privilege to be at the university at such a time.

Yet Bale seems to have been unmoved by the new learning. He progressed as he should through his studies: in the early 1520s he was ordained a priest and by the beginning of the 1530s he had gained his doctorate. His passion, however, lay mostly outside the university: the antiquities of the Carmelites. The history of the Order was his first love and during the 1520s he often left Cambridge to visit Carmelite houses in England, France and the Low Countries. He would scour their libraries, making extensive notes from manuscripts. Bale drew up a history of the Order, bringing together for the first time scattered historical texts, while remaining committed to the unproven, more mythical aspects of the Carmelites' rather hopeful understanding of their origins: Elijah, Elisha, Jonah and Isaiah were all listed as heads of the Order in its earliest and obscurest days. This may seem absurd to us but it reveals the central aspect of Bale's historical thinking. He considered the Carmelites to be the still turning point of the world; everything must relate to the Order even if there was no proof. Jonah must be a Carmelite because as a great prophet he must be a member of the greatest religious Order. Bale was a good antiquarian but his approach to history was not inductive; facts were made to fit with what he already believed.

Busy with manuscripts in the 1520s, Bale seems to have been untouched by ideas of religious dissension. A number of Lutherans, who would become highly prominent, were studying at Cambridge: Thomas Cranmer, the future Archbishop of Canterbury; Robert Barnes, an early and vocal English reformer, whose published attacks upon the papacy were at first appreciated by the Crown but who, as an associate of the king's secretary Thomas Cromwell, would be later destroyed by his fall; William Tyndale, who produced the first direct English translation of the Bible from Hebrew and Greek sources; and Miles Coverdale, who printed the first complete English translation of the Bible. Bale would later record that he knew Cranmer and Barnes at Cambridge but, at this stage, was not of their thinking. In fact, again and again, his writings at the time reveal a straightforward Catholic faith. In 1526, celebrating the Blessed Virgin Mary, whom he considered to be a Carmelite, Bale wrote: 'Hail flowering blossom of Carmel, the Father's pious daughter, Mother of Emmanuel, happy above thousands; O Virgin, give aid as you are wont, to your brothers. . . .' He took it for granted that celibacy and religious life were the superior state, noting that 'in the cell you will find what you most often lose outside.' And his writings upon the lives of Carmelite saints happily included the expected set miracles and virtues. No rumblings here of discontent. He would have to leave Cambridge to leave the Church.

At the beginning of the 1530s, Bale was made Prior of Maldon, Essex. It was a poor house and a backwater in Carmelite terms but he got stuck in and worked hard. In 1533, he became prior of the more substantial Carmelite Priory at Ipswich. It is there, back in his home county, that he was probably turned to Protestant ideas. Certainly, it is in Ipswich that he came to know the catalyst of his conversion: Thomas, first Baron Wentworth. This nobleman was born at Nettlestead in Suffolk. His grandfather, Sir James Tyrrel, had been executed as the alleged murderer of the princes in the Tower; his cousin, Jane Seymour, would become queen. By the end of the 1520s, he was recognised as someone who could be trusted to support the king's desire for a divorce from Queen Katherine and also back the Crown's early attacks upon the Church. To further both he was ennobled in 1529 so he could sit in the House of Lords. He was, however, more than just a supporter of the king but one of the first major figures in England to embrace Lutheran ideas. In Suffolk, he furthered the cause of the reformers whenever he could. Yet, notwithstanding his Protestantism, he presided over trials of men accused of denying transubstantiation rather than reveal too publicly and dangerously his own leanings.

For nearly thirty years, Bale had been a Carmelite and his Order was his love, but, whatever conversations he had with Wentworth or whatever writings Wentworth lent him or whatever people he introduced him to, soon after his arrival in Ipswich Bale's beliefs changed. He began to be persuaded by Protestant criticisms of the Mass and the saints. His wavering became a falling away after Henry VIII's direct attacks upon the papacy. In 1533, the year Bale arrived in Ipswich, Parliament passed the Act for Restraint of Appeals. This law, perhaps one of the most significant in English history, forbade all appeals to the pope on any issue and made the king the final legal authority on all matters, spiritual or temporal. The Act of Supremacy the next year was simply the logical development of this law. That it changed Bale is confirmed by him. He later wrote of Henry VIII that it was 'through his ministration that I am (as I hope) a partaker in God's Gospel kingdom, for before his edict against the Roman Pontiff, I was a very obstinate papist.'

By 1536 Bale was prior of the Carmelite House in Doncaster. He was now a Lutheran but he had not yet made the break. For two-thirds of his life he had been in religious vows; it was probably not easy to leave. He may have been unsure what to do. Should he use his position to further the cause of the Reformation? And what was the right thing to do regarding his vows? Were they still valid in this new world? But before the year ended he had made up his mind. Having moved to Thorndon in Suffolk to be the village's priest, he renounced his clerical vows, laid aside the religious habit and married a woman called Dorothy. He was behaving dangerously. Henry VIII may have started to act against the religious houses but he considered their vows still binding and clerical celibacy to be obligatory. Then, from Thorndon's pulpit, Bale preached against the veneration of saints and transubstantiation. Again, Henry VIII may have started to act against shrines as places of pilgrimage but he always upheld the worth of the saints as intercessors and the king was completely Catholic in his understanding of the Mass. Bale was denounced and ended up in custody in Greenwich. He was, however, rescued.

Thomas Cromwell was the king's principal secretary, chief minister and, regarding Church issues, his vicar general. He was, as long as he pleased the king, the most powerful man in the realm. Cromwell was also a religious reformer who pushed such policies as far as he could with a king who still wanted Catholicism but without the pope and with the wealth of the monasteries in the royal coffers. The king's principal secretary released Bale, protected him, and employed him to write propaganda against Rome – the now officially recognised home of the Antichrist.

Since the time of Pope St Gregory VII it had become usual for the papacy and the Holy Roman Empire, when they were in dispute, to accuse each other of being the Antichrist. In his writings, John Wyclif often identified Rome and certain popes from the eleventh century onwards, when papal political power grew, with Satan. Luther, however, taught that the very institution of the papacy and its holders since the reign of Boniface III in 607 were the Antichrist. Pope Boniface was the victim of Luther's ire because he had obtained from Emperor Phocas the decree that 'the See of Blessed Peter the Apostle should be the head of all the churches.' Henry VIII's government adopted this Antichrist rhetoric. From 1534 mendicant preachers were compelled by royal will to preach that the Bishop of Rome – you were no longer allowed to call him the pope – had no more authority than any other diocesan bishop and that his former power in the land had been usurpation. Bale's job was to be part of the propaganda machine, producing material, including plays, that consolidated these views of the papacy. This was not a hard job for Bale and when in the next few years he was to consider England and Wales' history, the corruption of the popes would be taken for granted.

Then, in 1540, Cromwell fell. The marriage he had arranged for Henry with Anne of Cleves had failed and the conservative faction at court had managed, even if for only a few weeks, to convince the king that Cromwell was treasonous. He was arrested in June and condemned to death. His execution was delayed but only so that he could testify to Henry's non-consummation of his marriage with the unfortunate Anne. Bale's own marriage and his association with Cromwell left him vulnerable – Robert Barnes was burned in July – so he fled with his family to Antwerp. The books he would produce whilst in exile would turn England's understanding of its own history upside down.

Antwerp was the second largest city north of the Alps and the most international. At different times it was home for exiles from Catholicism, Protestantism or, in Bale's case, Henry's own mixture of both. In this city of merchants, Bale sat down and wrote and in his writings he brought together two ideas: the already popular Lutheran identification of the papacy with the Antichrist and what Bale considered to be the key to understanding history – the Book of Revelation. St Augustine of Hippo had long ago taught, and Rome had for long maintained that the events in the last book of the Bible were not references to real historical moments but allegories for the hidden spiritual journey of the Christians. Since the 1200s, however, some had suggested that the Book of Revelation was about real historical events though in allegorical language. Bale accepted this notion completely and set about developing an understanding of Church history which he would later particularise to the Church in England and Wales.

In 1545, Bale produced a book entitled *The Image of Both Churches*. In it he argued that the seven seals referred to in chapters 6-8 of the Book of Revelation are seven periods of time since the Ascension. He then used these different periods to order the past and show how the purity of the early Church had been lost while God had always kept the truth – his Word – alive in a faithful few. The first seal was Pentecost and the Apostles' missions. The second was the first attacks on the earliest Christians. The third was the Church's loss of spiritual vigour after the time of Constantine. The beginning of the complete corruption of the Church, represented by the fourth seal, was, as Luther had argued but without recourse to the Book of Revelation, the award of the title of 'Universal Bishop' to Pope Boniface III by Emperor Phocas. Bale was struck by the closeness in time of Boniface's reign and the rise of Islam. He decided they were Gog and Magog (Revelation 20:8), the leaders of the forces that would oppress the faithful at the final loosing of Satan. It was at the time of the fourth seal, Bale noted, that corrupt practices such as the use of holy water had begun.

The fifth seal represented full-grown papal tyranny which persecuted true followers of God's Word and martyred them. This period of time stretched throughout Church history and enabled Bale to associate together different sects with sometimes very different, if not completely contrary, views. The beliefs of the Albigensians, for example, were not the same as those of the Waldensians but since they had both been denounced by Rome, the Antichrist, they must, according to Bale, both be true to the Gospel. As once Bale understood all historical events in relation to the Carmelites, now everything must be interpreted in the light of the faithful few and Satan's creature, the papacy. The sixth seal was the revival of the Gospel beginning with Wyclif's preaching in the 1370s. The Carmelites had been foremost in combating Wyclif; now a son of the Order was hailing him as the morning star of the Reformation.

This interpretation of Church history allowed Bale to present a timetable for the decline of the Roman Church; it was possible to show when things went wrong. The timetable must be right because it was allegedly forecast in the Bible. Until Constantine, opined Bale, the popes had been faithful preachers of the Word but after the great emperor, the light of the Gospel in the Church had gradually waned and gone, lasting only within a few poor souls in hidden corners. Satan had captured the Church completely in 1000 but already, since the early seventh century, the supposed Body of Christ had, in fact, been a false Church. It was not that morally the papacy was problematic with too many examples of popes whose lives had fallen short of the Gospel. According to Bale, the pope's depravity was theological and existential.

In *The Actes of Englysh votaryes,* published in two parts (1546 and 1551), Bale took his understanding of Church history and employed it solely upon the history of the Church in England and Wales. He *knew* that he would find the same Romanising corruption in this island. But before the centuries of Rome's tyrannical rule he discovered that England and Wales had been free and godly.

According to a popular tradition, Joseph of Arimathea brought Christianity to England in the year 63. Bale accepted this story but found within it a new significance: Joseph was a missionary from Jerusalem, not Rome. 'The Britons took the Christian faith at the very spring or first going forth of the Gospel, when the Church was most perfect, and had most strength of the Holy Ghost.' Things then began to decline because of the formation of dioceses, which introduced institutional rigidity, and the infiltration of monks who spread the belief that you could work out your own salvation. Next, in 597, the deadliest corruption arrived with the mission of St Augustine from Rome. For Bale, this monk was the minion of Antichrist, who introduced 'candlesticks, vestments, surplices, altar cloths, singing books, relics.' From their arrival, Bale wrote, these Roman monks laboured 'to prepare Antichrist a seat here in England, against the full time of his prefigured age, of 666.' The association of this number with the Antichrist is made in the Book of Revelation 13:18. According to Bale it was in the year 666 that St Theodore of Tarsus became the Archbishop of Canterbury, sent to finish what Augustine had begun. But here, as we shall see later with another historical figure, Bale allowed his view of how things must be to change how things were in fact. Whatever the significance of the number

666, it is not a date that connects St Theodore with England. He was appointed archbishop in 667, consecrated in Rome in 668, and arrived at Canterbury in 669. It is not that Bale wanted to mislead deliberately but he was so convinced that the pope was the Antichrist and the Book of Revelation a key not just to Church history in general but England and Wales' in particular, that he could make connections that, in truth, were not there.

Considering the missionaries from Rome, Bale also played the patriotic card and developed an idea which was consolidated during Elizabeth's reign: to be a true native of this isle is to be Protestant. Catholicism was dismissed as foreign. St Augustine and St Theodore, Bale argued, had established the Church of Rome only among the Saxon invaders, who a century or more before had pushed west the native British, who were of the Church founded by Joseph of Arimathea. This Church, the pure, uncorrupted one, continued but it was hidden and often survived in only a few individuals who could be identified because of their sufferings at the hands of Roman persecutors. True Church members, Bale wrote, are such as John Wyclif or, in contemporary England, William Tyndale and Robert Barnes. These men are the descendants of the earliest inhabitants in Britain. They are the visible remnants of the true Church, whose lineage stretches back, not to Rome, but to Jerusalem. With this argument, Bale attempted to dismiss much of England and Wales' history and rubbish most of their saints, such as St Boniface, St Edmund the Martyr and St Winefride, as servants of the Antichrist. Decades before the Spanish Armada, Bale was arguing that to be Catholic is to fall short of being British.

The second part of *The Actes of Englysh votaryes* covered merely the eleventh and twelfth centuries, but gave Bale room enough to show the Roman Church's increasing worldly ambition, reflecting Satan's complete mastery of her from the beginning of the new millennium. He argued that the clergy were the masterminds behind the foreign Norman invasion but then, as usual, unwilling to let kings legitimately rule, they opposed the new monarchs. St Thomas of Canterbury, therefore, was no martyr but a traitor. Bale had planned two other parts to *The Actes* but they were never written. They would have traced England's recovery from Wyclif to Henry VIII, a nation which unlike those of continental Europe had thrown off the thraldom of the Antichrist.

During the 1540s, inspired by the prophecies of Revelation, Bale had developed a new perception of the Church's history in England and Wales. He achieved this by destroying what had once been held dear in the nation's understanding of its own past, including the reputation of most of her saints. For the loss of England and Wales' saints, however, he had an answer: he created new ones. He began with the canonisation of Sir John Oldcastle. In 1544, Bale published in Antwerp a pamphlet about this knight so that the English and Welsh would know what a Protestant saint looked like. Oldcastle was burned for heresy in 1417. His religious views overlapped with many of the ideas that are collectively known as Lollardy, including anti-clericalism and identification of the pope with Antichrist. For Bale, here was proof of the hidden Church of the Britons made visible. But there were problems with Oldcastle. He had not only died for heresy but also for treason. When he was first found guilty of heresy he was not immediately condemned but sent to the Tower of London to give him time to reconsider his position. However, he promptly escaped and, at the beginning of 1414, led a small revolt and tried to kidnap the king, Henry V. It failed but he escaped and was on the run for three years until captured. Yet according to Bale's understanding of God's elect they always obey their divinely appointed rulers and had only ever resisted the pretensions of the Church. His response: the rebellion of Oldcastle must be a Romish fabrication; in truth, he died for the truth. Yet Oldcastle had other skeletons in the cupboard. He thought the pope was Antichrist but he was on record for belief in Purgatory. Again, Bale commented, this was fabrication. Despite obvious contradictions, Oldcastle was raised to the 'altar' of Protestant devotion. Bale's next subject, however, was a closer fit to type.

For many of Bale's readers, Oldcastle was a dim figure of the past but the smell of Anne Askew's burning flesh still lingered in the air of Smithfield. She had been executed in July 1546 for her Lollard beliefs on the nature of the Eucharist. The next year Bale published a history of her examination and burning. He presented her as a new kind of martyr, quite different from traditional Catholic expectations.

Askew was born around 1521, near Grimsby, into a family of comfortable means. She had an arranged marriage and gave birth to two children. Her relationship with her husband was strained; probably because of her conversion to Protestantism. In Lincolnshire she had become known for reading the Bible and her heretical ideas were suspected. Despite this she did not keep a low profile, but rather she did such things as publicly read from the Bible in Lincoln Cathedral. By 1544, perhaps seeking a legal separation, Askew had travelled to London. She quickly became known to the authorities there and the next year was questioned about her beliefs. She was released but remained under suspicion and during the summer of 1546 she was arrested and, this time, imprisoned. On 28 June, at Guildhall, Askew was found guilty of heresy and condemned to death. Meanwhile, conservative factions at court seemed to have been plotting against Henry's sixth wife, Katherine Parr, because of her support of the Reformation. Askew had family connections at court – her brother Edward was cup-bearer to the king – and she had occasionally joined the queen's Bible-reading circle. So though condemned and sentenced, Askew was taken to the Tower and racked to see if she would give any information that could be used against the queen or others at court. The chancellor, Sir Thomas Wriothesley, and a privy councillor, Sir Richard Rich, who had perjured himself to achieve the death of St Thomas More, were present as Askew was tortured and they may have even turned the rack. Yet Askew, if she had anything to give up, remained courageously silent. She was only twenty-five years old when she was eventually burned.

England and Wales' traditional and greatly loved saints included many martyrs who worked miracles and who as holy-helpers were often turned to in prayer. Henry VIII defended the celebration of saints but he allowed their role as intercessors for particular needs to be extinguished. In 1538, Cromwell issued a set of Injunctions which, whilst permitting the cult of saints, forbade public manifestations such as lighting candles before their images. He also encouraged the shortening or omission of litanies to saints in processions for the sake of succinctness.

With Anne Askew, Bale delivered a new kind of saint to fit in with this reformed understanding. She was a humble believer, a member of God's faithful who had witnessed to death; no miracle worker or new holy-helper. Bale, in writing about her, consciously presented himself as a modern day Eusebius, one of the Church's earliest martyrologists, thus linking Askew with the early, uncorrupted Church. This was the beginning of the dismissal of England's traditional Catholic martyrs. For Bale wrote, 'Bring St Edmund of Bury, St Fremund of Dunstable . . . and St Wynstave of Evesham (which are the best of the English martyrs) to the touch stone of God's Word and you shall find their martyrdoms and causes full unlike to theirs whom the bishops murder now apace in England.'

In considering Askew, Bale refined the argument he had begun in *The Actes of Englysh votaryes*. After the mission of Joseph of Arimathea, he argued, King Lucius had not sought the Christian faith from Pope Eleutherius, as had been popularly believed, but simply confirmation and rules for the further implementation of Christianity. Subsequent persecution during this period created true martyrs but St Emerita, the sister of King Lucius, St Alban, St Amphibalus, St Julius and St Aaron had died witnessing to an apostolic, not a papal, Church. They were known to be martyrs because they had been accompanied by the signs which Christ had promised to those of his disciples who took the faith to the pagan: 'They shall deliver you up in their counsels and synagogues. You shall be brought before rulers and kings, and be hated of all men in a manner for my name's sake' (Matthew 10:17-18). True martyrs, Bale declared, were not accompanied by miracles. Such works belonged to the Antichrist (Matthew 24:24). True martyrs were accompanied by the signs of persecution that Christ had predicted. This argument allowed Bale to dismiss every previously honoured saint who had lived since the arrival of St Augustine. Should Catholics respond with the counter-argument, 'But take note of their miracles,' Bale had a ready retort, 'See the sign of the Antichrist.' The traditional martyrs of England and Wales were dismissed as untrue, wicked or in St Thomas of Canterbury's case, manifestly treasonable.

One year after Edward VI's accession to the throne, Bale returned to England. Quite soon he met the younger John Foxe and for the rest of his life he encouraged, helped and inspired this future chronicler of the Protestant cause. In October 1552, Bale was appointed the Bishop of Ossory in Ireland. He spent seven months in Kilkenny preaching an unwanted reformed religion. When Mary came to the throne in 1553, his position became dangerous; one of his servants had already been killed for obeying Bishop Bale's order to work on a feast day. He fled from Dublin by ship, was taken prisoner by a Flemish man-of-war and eventually, through bribery, got himself to the Low Countries. Bale remained on the continent – his second exile – until the accession of Queen Elizabeth. His last years were spent at Canterbury; not quietly – for he sniffed out any Catholic tendencies – but he died peacefully enough in November 1563 and was buried in the nave of the cathedral of the city of St Augustine.

By the end of the 1540s, John Bale had done his principal work for the Protestant cause. He had established a non-Roman, non-papal foundation for the Church in England and Wales to which the Protestant martyrs witnessed by true signs. Henry VIII had thinned out the Calendar of the Saints. Of those who survived, Bale accused most of heresy, for in dying for the Roman faith they had deviated from the plain sense of the Scriptures. At least for now in propaganda terms, Bale had successfully undercut the Catholic Church. To the problematic question, 'Where was your Church before Luther?' he had formulated an answer: as prophesised by the Book of Revelation, she was often hidden, often persecuted but now becoming gloriously present in England and Wales, especially in her martyrs of the flames. It would be John Foxe who would become the great chronicler of the *true* church in England and its martyrs but, even before the burnings of Queen Mary, Bale had done all the hard work. It was now for the Catholic Church to respond. Yet she had already begun to do so thirty-five years before a nave flagstone hid Bale's body from the passing world.

Chapter 2

THE BLOCK AND THE STAKE

In 1528, the Cam, as ever, glided smoothly by and, perhaps, from his riverside priory, John Bale allowed himself time from theological and antiquarian pursuits to stop and stare. At Chelsea the waters of the Thames were bubbling, rushing by but Sir Thomas More may not have noticed. Busy with many things for the Crown, the Bishop of London had asked him to take on another commitment: read the heretical works coming into England and respond to them. More accepted, happily. The Thames could have been in full spate but he kept reading, especially the writings of William Tyndale.

Born in Gloucestershire around 1494, Tyndale studied at Oxford where he was ordained a priest. He had quickly showed a flair for languages and occupied himself with the recently published Greek New Testament. Such studies, and other influences we cannot trace, attracted him to Lutheranism and sowed an ambition in his heart: to produce an English translation of the Greek New Testament. Considering this an impossible dream to fulfil in England, he left for the continent and, in 1526, in the Lutheran city of Worms, his English New Testament drawing upon the latest learning was published. Some years before in Gloucestershire, upbraided by a man for his anti-papal thoughts, Tyndale had replied: 'I will cause a boy that driveth the plough, shall know more of the Scripture than thou dost.' Tyndale had remained true to that plough boy. The authorities in England became greatly concerned as copies of his New Testament began to reach our shores; without the mediation of the Church's ministers, who knew how lay people would presume to interpret for themselves the Word of God? The authorities were also alarmed by the explicit influence of Lutheran theology in Tyndale's translation. For example, in her translation of the

New Testament the Church employed the word 'priest' but Tyndale chose 'senior'. Such a change could be used to undermine the traditional understanding of the priesthood.

Tyndale, however, did not confine himself to translations. In the same year as his New Testament he wrote, again informed by Lutheranism, on St Paul's teaching of justification by faith. Then, in 1528 he produced two further blows aimed at Catholic doctrine. In *The Parable of the Wicked Mammon*, Tyndale attacked what he viewed as the Church's overemphasis on works to the detriment of faith and in *The Obedience of a Christian Man* he presented, for the first time in English, the two pillars of Reformation thought: the supreme authority of Scripture in the Church and, guided by Scripture, the supreme authority of the king over every subject, including every prelate. And these three works were not in the language of learned discussion – Latin – but in the language of the street and the field: English. We do not know the exact impact of Tyndale's writings but Anne Boleyn may have showed her *amour*, the king, a copy of *Obedience*, perhaps seeding a thought in his mind of a possible novel means to divorce.

More busied himself with these heretical writings, rarely putting down his pen and noticing the ever-flowing Thames, until the summer of 1529, when he had completed his first defence of Church teaching: *Dialogue Concerning Heresies*. It is written as a conversation between More and a student, beginning one day a little before seven in the morning in More's study at Chelsea. The student has read Tyndale and since his young mind is now veering to Martin Luther, he wants to hear a Catholic refutation. More refutes Tyndale, directly responding to his arguments and commenting that there have been heretics before who had 'left the common faith of the Catholic Church preferring their own gay glosses.' By the end of the day the student's confidence in holy Church has been re-established. More's work, however, was not done. In the autumn of 1529, Cardinal Wolsey fell from power – banished from the king's presence – and More replaced him as Lord Chancellor.

Three years later, the waters passing Chelsea's banks went once again unheeded. Tyndale had responded with *An Answer unto Sir Thomas More's Dialogue*. The Church, he declared, has perverted Scripture and is filled with corruption. Almost immediately, More must have begun his response. The days were now entirely occupied by his duties as Chancellor, his position was increasingly dangerous and isolated as he refused to condone any divorce from Queen Katherine, and his father died. Yet by the next year More had produced the first part of his *Confutation of Tyndale's Answer*. He took every point Tyndale had made in his writings, discussed them, challenged them and laid out Catholic doctrine, fully and exhaustively. He wrote with urgency fearing the old Faith was in great danger. He was right.

On 15 May 1532, after much royal harassment, the English Church's parliament – Convocation – passed *The Submission of the Clergy* in which it promised to make no laws without royal permission. In effect, it made the Crown supreme in all ecclesiastical matters. The next day and for the last time, Sir Thomas More met the king. What could he do now that the clergy had surrendered? He resigned as Lord Chancellor and bowed out. Free of official commitments, More finished the second part of his *Confutation*, fighting for the Church on paper if no longer in council. Yet before the king's lust swallows him up, it is time to see why More's four-year confrontation with Tyndale matters for us and our understanding of the wall paintings.

The reformers partially understood and defined themselves in relation to their sufferings at the hands of the Church and secular authorities. Persecution and martyrdom, as we have seen in Bale's writings, had become proof for them of their own righteousness. They were suffering for the Word of God, which Tyndale noted in the preface to *The Obedience of a Christian Man*, 'is ever hated of the world.' The Catholic Church as persecutor, therefore, is the 'world', the term often used in the New Testament for that which is opposed to God. The early reformers supported this view with the theological theory of the two Churches on earth – one visible and corrupt, the other invisible and true. The visible Church is the Catholic Church with its public acts of worship and power. The invisible Church is those who are truly godly and will be saved. Some members of the invisible Church are within the visible but because of persecution, most are outside, their righteousness hidden – that is, until the reformers uncovered it. Such an understanding enabled Tyndale and then Bale to portray very differing groups such as the Albigensians, Waldensians, Lollards and contemporary reformers as hidden remnants of the one, true Church. The Albigensians, who lived in southern France during the thirteenth century, were dualists, rejecting the flesh and all material creation as evil. The Waldensians, who emerged in the late-twelfth century in France, eventually denounced the Sacraments and supported lay preaching. The Lollards, a broad term covering many differing beliefs, opposed many elements of Church teaching while sometimes supporting doctrines, such as Purgatory, that later Protestant reformers would find embarrassing. Despite these differences, the reformers believed that martyrdom at the hands of the Church not only proved true godliness but was the golden thread that linked diverse groups together and created a new, alternative history of the true invisible Church.

Sir Thomas More responded to this theory in *Confutation*. He reiterated Catholic teaching on the Church: it is a universal, visible Christian community, with Christ its head and St Peter his Vicar 'and so forth the successors of him ever after.' By its very nature, therefore, it cannot be invisible and, as Bale would argue, local to England and Wales. The English and Welsh Church derives its legitimacy from its spiritual, historical and papal continuity with the rest of the universal Church. Yes, members of the Church, even popes, have been frail and fallen but that does not alter what the Church is: Christ's mystical body upon the earth. It is ridiculous, More wrote, to attempt to construct an invisible, true Church out of a group of heretics whose beliefs were so various and often contradictory. The Albigensians, Waldensians and Lollards represented not one Church but 'as many sects almost as men.' They had died not for the teachings of Christ but for the beliefs of their founders yet it is the cause for which you die, not the sufferings endured, which make you a martyr. St Augustine of Hippo had made this clear when, in the fourth century, he had denied the title martyr to Donatists killed for their schism. Equally, therefore, More declared, all these others who had died outside the Church while attacking it were not true martyrs. Cardinal Pole would later call them pseudomartyrs.

More also wrote of the witness of miracles. Christ had commanded his Apostles: 'Cure the sick, raise the dead, cleanse the lepers, cast out devils' (Matthew 10:8). In both *Dialogue Concerning Heresies* and *Confutation*, More argued that the many miracles associated with the saints, especially those of martyrs, proved the truth of Church teaching, which is partially founded upon their writings, and the truth of the Church itself, of which they were visible members and defenders, since such miracles were promised to his followers by Christ. This was simply to follow St Augustine of Hippo once more. In his great work *City of God*, he reports miracles from his own time, many of them in connection with the relics of martyrs, such as St Stephen, St Protasius and St Gervasius. The miracles happened, St Augustine writes, because either God worked through the 'spirits of the martyrs' or in answer to their prayers. They confirmed to pagans the truth of the Gospel: 'what do these miracles attest but the faith which proclaims that Christ rose in the flesh and ascended into heaven with the flesh?' And the miracles also attested to the martyrs themselves; they showed them to be authentic witnesses to God. In following St Augustine, More had presented an argument to counter Bale's future dismissal of many of England and Wales' saints, for had not these saints been attested to by miracles?

If More and Bale had met, however, they would have agreed on one thing: the followers of the Antichrist could also work miracles. More referred directly to Christ's prophecy '. . . false Christs and false prophets will arise and produce great signs and portents, enough to deceive even the chosen . . .' (Matthew 24:24). By the power of the Antichrist, More warned his readers, false martyrs – pseudomartyrs – would perform miracles. Perhaps he had heard about such incidents as the public burning of the works of Martin Luther in Germany in 1521. Afterwards, in the ashes, a woodcut of the reformer was found completely unharmed. This was immediately hailed by some followers as miraculous. And John Foxe, the author of *Acts and Monuments* (immediately popularly known from its first edition in 1563 as his *Book of Martyrs*), differed from Bale, his senior colleague and mentor, by recording many miracles linked to Protestant martyrs. But such wondrous doings, wrote More, could not be trusted as a sign of God's blessing. The heretics may seem holy because of their fasting, almsgiving and courageous suffering but having left the Church they are forerunners of the Antichrist. They may even die like true martyrs but they are of 'the devil's martyrs'. Future generations of English Catholics, in writing and in paint, would use More's writings both to defend from Bale's scorn the miracles of England and Wales' saints – and so the saints themselves and their support of the papacy – and to dismiss, or attribute to the Antichrist, the miracles of the persecuted reformers lovingly recorded by Foxe. Our wall paintings are both such a defence and a dismissal. Fifty years later, informed by More's confrontation with Tyndale, the paintings defended the visibility of the true Church and its synonymy with the ancient Catholic Church in England and Wales by making her history visible in paint. And they also dismiss Protestant martyrs and Bale's attack upon miracles by depicting Catholic martyrs and their abundant miracles.

One of the depicted Catholic martyrs is Sir Thomas More. On 13 April 1534, two years after he had resigned as Lord Chancellor, More refused to swear to the Act of Succession. He had no doubts that parliament could decide the line of succession but the oath also involved recognising other legislation such as the Act for Restraint of Appeals, which denied the pope's authority. This More would not do. He was sent to the Tower of London for one last year of life. Even during those hard imprisoned months, More kept on writing, bolstering himself in the face of death with meditations upon Christ's passion while also continuing his confutation of Master Tyndale. He was martyred, dying calmly and wittily – the king's good servant but God's first – on 6 July 1535.

Tyndale survived More by only a year. Though he was now living in Antwerp, within the lands ruled by the staunch defender of the Catholic faith, Emperor Charles V, the City Fathers did little to interfere with foreign guests, not wishing to damage trade. Tyndale's writings and presence, however, were brought to the attention of the Emperor's court by an Englishman, Henry Phillips, who may have been employed by an English bishop but was certainly motivated by the hope of a reward of money. Tyndale was arrested in May 1535 and imprisoned for over a year in the castle of Vilvorde, often questioned and probably poorly treated. In August 1536, he was condemned as a heretic for his Lutheranism, publicly degraded from the priesthood, including the symbolic scraping of the chrism from his hands, and in October, in a square of Vilvorde, he was strangled to death and his body consumed by fire. Thomas Cromwell tried to save Tyndale but had he remained in England Henry VIII would probably have burned him. As More and Tyndale suffered death, John Bale was in Ipswich, under the reforming influence of Lord Wentworth. Yet it was More, before Bale had even picked up a pen, who in challenging Tyndale had already begun to refute the arguments our Carmelite would make. And it is More's counter-arguments that had begun to shape the story told by the wall paintings of the English College.

Chapter 3

THE CARDINAL

It is not a particularly Christian observation but some families seem to be pursued by the Furies. George, the Duke of Clarence, drowned in a butt of malmsey. His daughter, Blessed Margaret Pole, the Countess of Salisbury, was hacked to pieces at the execution block. Her eldest son, Henry, Baron Montagu, was beheaded. The truth, of course, is that it is dangerous to stand too close to the Throne. Fortunately for Reginald Pole, unlike the rest of his family, he kept his distance until it was safe, indeed, wonderful to approach.

Born in 1500, Pole was the great-nephew of the Kings Edward IV and Richard III, through his grandfather, the Duke of Clarence, who suffered execution by sweet wine for antagonising his brother, Edward, too many times. Pole's mother, Margaret, was married off by Henry VII after he had defeated her uncle Richard at Bosworth. She eventually became a great friend and loyal supporter of Katherine of Aragon and also a considerable landowner. On his father's side, however, Reginald Pole was a kinsman of Henry VIII. So despite his dubious Yorkist pedigree he was favoured by the king, who sponsored his studies first at Oxford and then Padua. In the late 1520s, Pole repaid this kindness by supporting the divorce and persuading the University of Paris to do the same. But during the first half of the 1530s, having returned to Italy, he had a conversion experience; his living faith in Christ and the Catholic Church blossomed and would never die. So when he received the news in the summer of 1535 of the executions of both John Fisher, the Bishop of Rochester, and Thomas More he was horrified. At the same time, Thomas Cromwell, perhaps ignorant or fearful of Pole's change of heart, wrote to him demanding his support for the Royal Supremacy. Pole's response to the king's chief minister was his only book published during his lifetime: *Pro Ecclesiasticae Unitatis Defensione* (normally referred to as *De Unitate*).

Addressing Henry directly, Pole presented a powerful theological defence of papal primacy, citing three scriptural passages: Matthew 16:18, 'You are Peter and on this rock I will build my Church'; John 21:15, 17, 'Feed my lambs . . . feed my sheep'; and Luke 22:32, '. . . I have prayed for you, Simon, that your faith may not fail.' The authority which Christ had bestowed upon this fisherman, Pole explained, had passed to his successors: the bishops of Rome. This authority cannot be usurped because the Church, the universal People of God, is united in and through the papacy. So Henry VIII's actions are nothing more than those of an ageing man for the 'love of a harlot' and a greedy tyrant desiring the Church's goods. Pole had rightly focused upon the only question that mattered: from what we find in Scripture had it been Christ's intention to found the office of the papacy? Pole's scriptural presentation was clear: Christ had intended the papal ministry. Yet Pole went beyond biblical exegesis and also considered the evidence of English history.

Bale, eleven years later in his work on Anne Askew, will try to reduce the pope's importance in English history by arguing, contrary to Bede's account, that the second-century King Lucius had not sought the Christian faith from Rome but merely rules for the further implementation of an already-established Christianity. And in *The Actes of Englysh votaryes*, he will describe St Augustine's mission as a corruption of the English and Welsh Church. In *De Unitate*, however, Pole presented a history of England that emphasised the providential role of the papacy in the country from the earliest days of the Church. He reminded Henry VIII that, according to Bede, Christianity itself – not just rules – had been brought to our island at the time of King Lucius by missionaries, who had been sent by Pope Eleutherius at the request of the king. Pole also celebrated Augustine of Canterbury's mission in 597 which, at the instigation of Pope Gregory, had converted the Saxons and so begun the restoration of Christianity throughout England and Wales.

Pole then turned to the contemporary witness of More and Fisher. They were legates from God to England, whose credentials were written in blood. In defying your illegitimate claims, Pole told Henry, they had died as martyrs in defence of the unity of the Church. Their deaths were proof, in themselves, of the centrality of papal authority. And not letting the king off the hook, Pole observed that God 'has sent us books against your deceitful wisdom . . . we have these writings from the finger of God, the very holy martyrs of God . . . a certain book written not with ink but with blood.' Pole recognised their deaths for the cause of Church unity and the authority of the pope as a particular divine blessing upon England, for such martyrdoms had not been granted to any other country afflicted by religious division. Bale would present his own historical arguments for a national Church independent of Rome but such an institution was, for scriptural and historical reasons, inconceivable to Pole, as it had been to More. The Church is one and visible, in union with Peter, or no Church at all.

Pole sent *De Unitate* to the king in May 1536. Cromwell, in response, demanded that Pole return to England. But he would not return until after eighteen years of high drama on the continent and at the centre of the life of the Church. In December, having called him to Rome, the Pope, Paul III, appointed Pole a cardinal and a few months later gave him responsibility for supporting any uprisings against King Henry. Pole was now, therefore, one of the greatest threats abroad to his kinsman. Several English-sponsored assassins tried to kill the cardinal but his minders were watchful. Then, from 1538, Pole was charged with preparing a General Council for the Church and in the same year he was made head of the English Hospice in Rome, which would later become the English College. Pole's family in England, however, suffered for his defiance of the king and his meteoric rise in the Church. In the summer of 1538, his brother Geoffrey was arrested for his supposed complicity in what became known as the Exeter Conspiracy, a purported attempt to kill the king and replace him with a Yorkist heir. Geoffrey may not have been entirely mentally balanced: his testimony led to the execution of his innocent brother, Henry, and the imprisonment of his equally innocent mother. Margaret Pole was kept in the Tower until the spring of 1541 but the suspected plots of the cardinal against Henry, her lands on the south coast (a perfect site for an invading army to land), and her claim to the throne made her too dangerous in the king's mind. On 27 May 1541 she was beheaded. Pole's reaction to the news of his mother's death was recorded by his secretary. The cardinal immediately declared himself to be the proud son of a martyr and consoled his stricken secretary by reassuring him that he now had 'one more advocate in paradise.' Pole then withdrew to his oratory and an hour later 'came out as cheerful as before.'

For the cardinal, the 1540s were taken up by preparations for the Council of Trent, the first sessions of the Council and the government of papal lands. And then, at the very end of the decade, Paul III died and during the conclave to choose his successor, Pole came only two votes short of being elected pope. It was probably his refusal to do anything to advance his own candidacy which denied him this supreme office. But then Pole had spent his time in the conclave writing a treatise which argued that the only acceptable candidate for the papacy was one who did not want it. It was this humility and true love of Christ which made him so popular. Then, in 1553 – and it seemed a miracle to many, Protestants as well as Catholics – Katherine of Aragon's daughter, Mary, came to the throne of England. After twenty years of royal supremacy, Catholicism would be restored and Cardinal Pole would be the Crown's and the papacy's instrument of that restoration.

It was a sight that had not been seen since the days of Cardinal Wolsey of unhappy memory. On the evening of 30 November 1554, Cardinal Pole, in full pontificals, was conducted from Lambeth Palace across the River Thames by six Garter Knights. At Westminster, by the light of torches – the sun having set – he was presented by Queen Mary and her husband, King Philip, with a petition from Parliament asking absolution for the kingdom's schism. All present, including the monarchs, then knelt down as the cardinal, as Legate of the Vicar of Christ, read out a brief formula beginning:

> Our Lord Jesus Christ, which with his precious blood has redeemed us, and purified us of all our sins and pollutions, in order to make himself a glorious bride without stains and without wrinkle, whom the Father made chief over the Church, he through his mercy absolves you.

And having been blessed in the name of the Father and the Son and the Holy Spirit, cries of 'Amen' rang out from all sides. Edward VI on the day of his death had prayed that England might be saved from papistry but, instead, by the hands of his kinsman, it was restored.

Two days before, having only just returned to England after an absence of eighteen years, Pole had addressed Parliament. After describing the evil consequences of England's break with Rome, the cardinal noted that Henry's actions had overturned the country's special place in history, for under King Lucius it had been the first kingdom 'by the public consent of kings and people to accept the faith.' Since then England had been

cared for by the popes, and in return had given 'singular obedience
. . . unto their father in faith the Pope of Rome.' Moreover, they had
exported this obedience: English missionaries had brought to Northern
Europe both Christianity and fidelity to the Holy See. Great, therefore,
was the fall when Henry denied the Vicar of Christ yet England, unlike
countries in the East, whose repudiation of papal authority had led to
their occupation by the Turks, had miraculously recovered under Mary.
The reason for this miracle, Pole told Parliament, was the Catholic
martyrs of Henry's reign, whose deaths had prevented the country from
entirely abandoning the Church. As the blood of Christ's death had
saved us, 'so the blood of those his servants whom the guilty put to
death, have been a means to bring you to this mercy . . . that you might
be such as they were in faith and constancy, and in participation of
God's grace.' Thomas More the Traitor had become Thomas More the
Martyr.

Pole developed this vein of thought further. Repeating from *De
Unitate* his comparison of the blood of martyrs with ink, he said to
Parliament that neither the preaching of the early English missionaries,
nor all the books ever written, 'have given so much light of truth and
of true catholic doctrine, as God has written to you and to all the
world in their blood.' This was a singular 'honour, pre-eminence and
dignity,' for in a time in which 'the Catholic faith having been and yet
still being persecuted in diverse countries and nations, yet have we not
before heard of any that in these late years have died for the unity of
the Church, which is the maintenance of the true faith and religion.'
As Bale had held up England as a unique model of the true reformed
Church, so now Pole held up England as a unique witness, through her
martyrs, to Church unity. Looking back to the papal foundations of the
Church, the cardinal told Parliament that by returning to the Church
they would show themselves 'a similitude of such persons as in the
primitive church were called to this grace, in so great abundance of the
gift of God's spirit, that your notable example in this behalf might be,
as it were, a second foundation of his most glorious Catholic Church, to
other nations.' What a vision! England's witness, as in the times of the
Saxon missionaries, would blaze forth to the rest of Europe and restore
those nations that still strayed from Catholic unity.

Almost exactly four years after Pole's address to Parliament – short by
only one day – Queen Mary died in the morning and the cardinal in the

evening. Their too brief reigns as Monarch of England and Archbishop of Canterbury – extinguished, as it were, with one diurnal breath – left the restored Catholic Church vulnerable. It was quickly blown away by the new Queen, Elizabeth. Catholics would soon have to compromise, suffer or go into exile. John Bale, however, could return to take up residency in Canterbury.

Yet Pole, from 1536 in *De Unitate*, had successfully established and propagated an understanding of English Church history which, countering Bale's, emphasised the role of the papacy: from Pope Eleutherius' mission to King Lucius, through the reconversion by Pope Gregory, to the Saxon kings' loyalty to the Holy See and the Saxon missionaries' spreading of unity with that See. Thomas More's writings had already provided a defence of the visible Church and a proper understanding of martyrdom and miracles. And now Pole could point to More himself, holding him up to England and Europe as a new type of martyr, whose death witnessed to the necessity of the Office of Peter for Christian unity. The influence of Pole's presentation of Church history in England upon the wall paintings of the English College is apparent: King Lucius, including his baptism by the pope's legates, is the subject of the second picture; St Gregory's sending of St Augustine is celebrated; English missionaries spreading the Faith, including loyalty to the papacy, in northern Europe in the 700-800s are depicted; and most extraordinarily, as a sort of coup for Pole's thinking – an event never referred to by the cardinal – the first picture shows the first pope, St Peter himself, coming to England.

And throughout, the wall paintings show, in lurid scenes, the continuity of martyrdom in English and Welsh history. The first twenty-four pictures are principally the martyrs, often martyred missionaries, of England and Wales' first thirteen hundred years of Christianity. They are accompanied by miracles, attesting, as More taught, to the genuineness of the martyrdoms. But then the twenty-fifth picture depicts the executions of More, Fisher and Cardinal Pole's mother. The link, the continuity is clear: the earliest martyrs and the most recent had died for the same cause – the faith of the Church, including its teaching of the authority of the divinely-instituted papacy.

Chapter 4

A CHALLENGE

St Paul's Cross has been described as *The Times* newspaper of the Middle Ages. It was a raised wooden, lead-covered pulpit, which stood in the grounds of St Paul's Cathedral from which thousands were often addressed on the most important issues of the day. It was where London gathered to hear announcements of victories, royal marriages and excommunications and, during the sixteenth century, it was the focal point of religious controversy. There Tyndale's translation of the Bible was burned; there Henry VIII had papal authority preached against; there, during Mary's reign, Protestantism was denounced. The pulpit was destroyed during the English Civil War – a memorial now marks the spot – and today, where thousands once stood, City workers eat their cellophane-wrapped lunches. But in its heyday, on 26 November 1559, just a year after the deaths of Queen Mary and Cardinal Pole, St Paul's Cross witnessed the issuing of a great challenge.

John Jewel, Bishop-Elect of Salisbury, standing in the pulpit, preached on the Eucharist. He declared that the new Elizabethan liturgical practices, which had just replaced the Mass, were in continuity with the practices of the early Church while the Catholic use of the Latin language, communion under one kind, the canon of the Mass, 'the adoration of the Sacrament', the practice of private Masses, and other such matters as papal primacy, were abuses not found in ancient times. Having claimed, therefore, continuity for the reformed Church of England with the Early Church, Jewel finished his sermon with this challenge:

> If any one of all our adversaries be able clearly and plainly to prove, by such authority of the scriptures, the old doctors, and councils . . . I am content to yield unto him, and to subscribe. But I am well assured that they shall never be

able truly to allege one sentence. And because I know it, therefore I speak it, lest you happily should be deceived.

Jewel's 'Challenge' was a gauntlet which many Catholic apologists took up but, perhaps, none of them did so more successfully than Thomas Stapleton. He was a great scholar and prolific author; by 1640 there were more than 140 editions of his various writings. Popes Gregory XIII and Clement VIII had his works read aloud at meals. Gregory particularly liked to listen to Stapleton's *Antidota apostolica*, commentaries on Acts and St Paul's Epistles, which explained how Protestants had twisted their meaning. Stapleton was named in honour of Thomas More, having been born only a few days after the martyr's execution into a family who opposed the king's actions against papal authority. He studied at Oxford, became a fellow of New College and, early in 1558, was ordained a priest. In that same year, however, Elizabeth came to the throne and there was soon a purge of Oxford, the University being considered too Catholic after Mary's reign. Like so many other Catholic scholars, Stapleton fled abroad and settled in the Low Countries. Except for a brief return home, he was to remain an exile for the rest of his life. Yet again, like many of his fellow exiles, he worked tirelessly for the restoration of Catholicism in England and Wales. His particular contribution was the written word and, as part of this, he published in 1565 his translation of Bede's *Ecclesiastical History of the English People*. The *History* is not, in itself, a controversial work but Stapleton's translation of it and the appendix he added were a direct response to Jewel's challenge for proof of Catholic continuity.

St Bede the Venerable, a monk of Jarrow monastery and one of the most learned men of his time, had written his Latin history of Christianity in England in 731. It commenced with the invasion of Julius Caesar and continued to his own day. It was the principal chronicle of the early Church in England and was considered trustworthy by both Protestants and Catholics. Bale and Foxe happily used Bede but, according to Stapleton, Bede's *History* disproved Jewel. The title of an appendix by Stapleton of almost five hundred pages, published with the *History*, succinctly expresses his understanding of Bede's take on the Church in England: *A fortresse of the faith first planted among us Englishmen, and continued hitherto in the universall*

church of Christ. The faith of which time Protestants call, papistry.
There you have it, says Stapleton: Catholicism, not Protestantism,
is continuous with the early Church. Bede, as his translator knew,
stressed the essential involvement of the papacy in the founding of
the Church in England, beginning with King Lucius' request for
missionaries from Pope Eleutherius. However, the Church really
developed, according to Bede, with St Augustine's arrival from Rome.
And from England it spread to other countries; as the full title of
Stapleton's appendix recalls, in the phrase *'the faith first planted among
us Englishmen and continued hitherto in the universall church,'* Bede
gives many examples of Saxon missionaries going to Northern Europe
to spread Christianity. Therefore, to summarise Stapleton's argument,
what Rome teaches today is what the English Church believed from
the beginning since the Church in England was founded principally
by Rome and taught to other countries fidelity to Rome.

In *A fortresse*, having challenged Jewel by listing forty-four
differences between Protestant belief and 'the primitive Faith of
England continued almost these thousand years', as recorded in
Bede, Stapleton is particularly critical of John Bale or as he variously
calls him: 'Bawdy Bale', 'that swinish heretic', and 'foul-mouthed
ruffian.' Bale had constructed an invisible true Church on earth, but
Stapleton responds that the true Church must be 'of necessity always
. . . a clear, evident, visible, and known Church' in order that it might
be recognised. The martyr Edmund Campion, depicted in the wall
paintings, would also stress this point. In his own written challenge
to Protestants, *Decem Rationes*, which was secretly printed in England
in 1581, he listed ten reasons for believing in the Catholic Church.
His third reason was that Protestants had destroyed the nature of the
Church. Unable to trace their theological pedigree, he argued, they
claimed a Church 'all hidden away'. The Church had ceased, therefore,
in their hands to be a visible, historical entity, becoming invisible
except to the few. The wall paintings, in themselves, therefore, argue
this point, for what could be more visible than paintings? By simply
including many episodes of Bede's *History* in its painted presentation
of English and Welsh history, the college visibly showed the historical
and continual visibility of the Catholic Church in England and
Wales. The fact that you could paint it proved it was true. So it is not
surprising that at the college in Douai, founded in 1569 as the first

seminary for Englishmen, the students had to study Bede as part of their syllabus. As their Rector, William Allen, said, it provided them with a 'very telling argument'.

In *The Actes of Englysh votaryes*, published in 1554, Bale had described a British Church, founded by Joseph of Arimathea, free of Rome's corruption. Bede never referred to Joseph; his involvement in British history was only mentioned some hundreds of years later by the fabulist Geoffrey of Monmouth. But his founding role was fondly accepted by many, Protestant and Catholic, in England. Bale's version of English history in the years after Joseph has the true Church becoming increasingly invisible as it is pushed west by pagan Angle and Saxon invaders. These interlopers' subsequent conversion at the behest of Pope Gregory created, Bale argued, a new corrupt English Church.

Stapleton's response to this was simple: he stuck with Bede. Ignorant of any real knowledge of the Church before St Augustine's mission except for Bede's brief references to King Lucius or the martyr St Alban, he wrote that the true Church was the 'catholic faith planted among Englishmen by holy St Augustine our Apostle.' Augustine's missionaries on arrival worked 'to reduce the old Britons to the unity of Christ's Church.' But whatever did exist in England between the time of the Apostles and St Augustine, Stapleton argued that its 'doctrine and ecclesiastical government agreed and concurred with the practice and belief' of the rest of the Church; the ancient Britons had been part of the visible papal Church, for King Lucius had requested missionaries from Pope Eleutherius. Our wall paintings, as well as being influenced by Pole, also seem to be informed by this debate. They focus on the English (Saxon) Church, but, even before the arrival of St Augustine, the Church in England is already loyal to Rome: Lucius is depicted kneeling before Eleutherius' legates, and Constantine, acclaimed Emperor first in England, kneels before the pope.

Stapleton clashed with Bale over one other issue: miracles. Bale had dismissed the miracles of the saints as works of the Antichrist, but the Gospels had promised that they would be a sign to pagans to aid their conversion, and again and again in Bede miracles are worked as Christianity is established in England and abroad. In the sixteenth century, miracles remained important to the Church. The former Protestant, Laurentius Surius, informed by the latest good practices of historical research, published six volumes of hagiography in Cologne from 1570-1575. He included 699 saints and, perhaps surprisingly, 6,538 miracles because, as he explained, they are an identifying mark of the true Church.

Stapleton knew this well. In *A fortresse*, miracles were at the top of his list of forty-four differences between Catholics and Protestants: Catholics had them, Protestants did not. And, like others before him, he would ridicule the improbable details of miracles that Foxe claimed for his Protestant martyrs. Stapleton later wrote in his *Tres Tomae* (1588):

> Let then this be the first difference gathered out of this history. That in the planting of the papist's faith and religion God has wrought miracles. In the planting of the Protestants' doctrine no miracles appear . . . For as the miracles of Foxe in his *Acts and Monuments*, his own fellows esteem them but as civil things.

So for Stapleton, Bede's many references to miracles prove that the preaching of St Augustine and his successors was authentic and blessed by God and that Rome's emissary was founding a true Church in England, for miracles are given for the sake of pagans that 'good life in such as newly receive the faith is more fervent.' Many miracles are noted in the wall paintings. They defend the depicted saints from Bale's libel and, as in Stapleton's *A fortresse*, link the Catholic Church with the true Church. From the painting of Thomas More's death onwards, however, there are no references to the miraculous. In the early centuries of English history miracles had been proof of the establishment of the true Church among the pagans but, in the scenes recording historical events from 1535 onwards, their absence indicates that the martyrs of Henry and Elizabeth are true martyrs dying for the already established true Church and its unity.

John Jewel, having become the enthroned Bishop of Salisbury and a valued member of the Elizabethan establishment, died in 1571. He was buried in Salisbury Cathedral in the middle of the choir opposite the bishop's throne. Thomas Stapleton, having been made a protonotary, an important office in the curia, by his admirer Pope Clement VIII, died in exile at Louvain in the autumn of 1598. Two years after his translation of Bede, Stapleton had written in a new work, *Counterblast*, what he and other Catholic refugees hoped in vain might happen:

I trust the queen's majesty, once considering, will graciously bear with the Catholics that do not envy [her titles], but only desire that their consciences may not be straitened for one of them. Which they upon great grounds and they verily think without impairing of her worldly estate, cannot by oath assuredly avouch; which thing they trust they may do without any just suspicion of sedition or rebellion.

Interlude

Robert Abbot, Master of Balliol College, Oxford, mused in 1611, in his work of controversy, *The True Ancient Roman Catholike,* that those seeking assurance of faith 'cannot study the chronicles for the finding of it.' As a strict Calvinist he was suspicious of humane studies but noted fairly the potential problem with histories: 'we may rather gather from them the private affection of the author, then any testimony of public faith.' With *sola scriptura* as their creed, Protestants were always going to be suspicious of any authorities apart from Holy Writ. And Catholics would have agreed with Pole's approach in *De Unitate*: begin with the Petrine texts in the Gospels. But history is where scriptural passages are lived out or not; passing time has its own insights to give. And the battle over historical understanding, which we have traced for four chapters, was there from the very beginning of the English Reformation. The preamble to the Act in Restraint of Appeals of April 1533, which, in effect, gave Henry VIII supremacy over the Church, begins: 'Where by divers sundry old authentic histories and chronicles it is manifestly declared and expressed that this realm of England is an empire. . . .' With this fantastical historical assertion that his crown was imperial, Henry claimed an authority over the Church in his country, which no emperor before him had sought. The king made history the battlefield.

John Bale, antiquarian Carmelite turned Protestant bishop, delighted in history. In the preface to his life of Sir John Oldcastle, he wrote of the need to 'set forth' English chronicles, which was the most essential 'thing to be laboured to the honour of God . . . next the Sacred Scriptures of the Bible.' John Foxe, in the preface to *Acts and Monuments*, wrote of his feelings when he saw the misery of Christ's flock 'all for ignorance of history, not knowing the course of the times and true descends of the church, it pitied me.' So they wrote history; Bale in the light of the Book of Revelation, Foxe by the light of Smithfield's fires. And because their histories would have made the visible Catholic Church, her saints and the popes, the creatures of the Antichrist, if not the Antichrist itself,

Pole, Stapleton and many others fought back with history. Inspired by More, the increasing number of martyrs and over a thousand years of Catholic England and Wales, they wrote, lived in exile, and suffered imprisonment to defend a correct and true account of the ecclesiastical history of the English and Welsh people. The wall paintings in the English College are part of this great defence and they cannot be fully appreciated without an understanding of the debate that required such a defence. As a response to Bale, the mythmaker, the aim of the paintings could be aptly described by Cardinal Newman's gravestone epitaph: *ex umbris et imaginibus in veritatem* – from shadows and appearances into truth.

The prize for the successful claimant of the origins of the English and Welsh Church was potentially great. What was at stake is apparent in something as seemingly insignificant as clerical jeering in Oxford. William Laud, the future Archbishop of Canterbury, was rounded upon by Robert Abbot in an Easter sermon in 1615. Abbot, believing Laud's Calvinism to be deficient, demanded, before a full congregation, to know of him whether he were 'Romish or English? Papist or Protestant?' That was the rub. Bale and Stapleton were not fighting for the past but for the present. What were we according to our birthright, Catholic or Protestant? The wall paintings are a rallying cry to the students of the college to seize back for the Church what had long been hers: England and Wales.

Chapter 5

SALVETE FLORES MARTYRUM

In Rome in 1578, a group of workmen were digging away, filling their barrows with pozzolana; perhaps the volcanic rock was needed for concrete in one of the pope's many new educational establishments. Gregory XIII knew that reform of the Church was impossible without well-educated priests. He had reconstructed and endowed the Roman College, secured the future of the German College and, though she already existed as an established community, in a year's time the English College would be formally founded by papal bull. And that's not to mention Gregory's other projects: the Greek, Maronite, Armenian and Hungarian Colleges. So one day workmen were digging away for Italian rock (perhaps to build up the church in foreign lands – volcanic soil has always been fertile) when the ground beneath their feet suddenly collapsed and the men found themselves falling into the second century.

This extraordinary discovery of the catacomb of St Priscilla mesmerised Rome. The long-lost catacomb had been used as a burial place for the Christian dead, including seven early popes and many martyrs, from the second to the fifth century. Cesare Baronius, the contemporary Church historian, wrote:

> All of Rome was filled with wonder, for it had no idea that in its neighbourhood there was a hidden city, filled with tombs of the days of the persecutions of the Christians. That which we knew before from written accounts and from a few cemeteries which were only partially opened out, we can now realise fully, and filled with wonder, see with our own eyes the confirmation of the accounts of St Jerome and Prudentius.

Another commentator noted that 'men can picture to themselves the persecutions, the sufferings and the piety of the saintly members of the primitive Church.' And, most interestingly for us, he concludes, 'it is obviously a further confirmation of our Catholic religion.' The bones of those who were thought to be martyred did not remain long in their burial places; new relics were soon gracing Rome's altars. The City of St Peter and St Paul was quickly becoming the City of Many Martyrs.

An influential promoter of devotion to the early martyrs was St Philip Neri. Born in Florence in 1515, he studied in Rome and spent many years in the city as a layman, dedicating himself to prayer and care of the needy. In his late thirties he was ordained a priest and became a hugely popular pastor because of his faith and humour, gentleness and charisma. Many Roman citizens sought his guidance; successive popes honoured him. From his earliest days in Rome, St Philip had spent entire nights in prayer in the catacomb of St Sebastian, drawn to it as a resting place of the martyrs. He encouraged this devotion in others, leading crowds of people around the churches of Rome which were associated, in particular, with the martyrs while encouraging scholars to study the catacombs. The students of the English College shared St Philip's devotion. Anthony Munday, a future playwright, was staying at the college in 1578 when the catacomb of St Priscilla was rediscovered. We do not know whether, at the time, he was a sincere Catholic or merely dissembling but only a few years later in England he would testify against Catholic priests at their trials. On the day the students made their own visit to the catacomb, Munday was, as he wrote, 'lying sick in my bed' but he records the students' enthusiasm after their visit. They told him 'what a heavenly place it was, what a number of saints and martyrs had been buried there, and what precious relics were daily found there.'

The students, however, would be able to look increasingly among themselves for acts of martyrdom. Ralph Sherwin, the first recorded student of the English College, was also its first martyr. In 1581, with Munday acting as a witness for the Crown, Sherwin was found guilty of treason and on 1 December he was hanged, drawn and quartered at Tyburn. When word of his execution reached Rome, the students sang a hymn praising God, the *Te Deum*; a tradition they subsequently maintained on hearing the news of other martyrdoms. If they were sad for the loss of a companion, the students were, as Cardinal Pole had been on hearing of the execution of his mother, proud and thankful for a new martyr; the death was not a failure but a divine blessing. St Philip Neri saw in the students of the English College the early martyrs *redivivi*. When he met them in the street, he would greet the students with words borrowed from the early Christian poet Prudentius: 'Salvete flores martyrum' – 'Hail flowers of the martyrs'. St Philip believed that the Faith and Church they were willing to die for was no different from the Faith and Church for which the first Christians had died. These English men were the unbroken link in the chain to the earliest martyrs of Rome.

Chapter 6

THE SOCIETY OF JESUS

Above the altar in the church of the English College hangs a painting called the Martyrs' Picture. It was painted in 1581 for that spot. It depicts the Most Holy Trinity: God the Father holds the crucified body of his incarnate Son, with the Holy Spirit, in the form of a dove, hovering between them. Below, two martyred English saints pray in adoration: St Thomas of Canterbury and St Edmund the Martyr. It is not their presence which gives the picture its name but the college's tradition of singing the *Te Deum* before it on the news of a former student's martyrdom. Below the feet of Christ, an angel holds a banner inscribed with the words: *Ignem veni mittere in terram*. It is Jesus' declaration about himself as recorded in the Gospel of St Luke – 'I have come to bring fire to the earth' (12:49) – and its inclusion in the painting tells us everything. This scriptural quotation was a favourite of the founder of the Society of Jesus (the Jesuits), St Ignatius of Loyola. He often finished his letters with the inspiring message: *Ite inflammate omnia* – 'Go and set the world on fire!' The English College was not a Jesuit foundation nor did it ever become a Jesuit house but for the first two hundred years of its history, its spirituality and culture were formed by the Society.

After a difficult beginning in 1578 with its first rector, a Welsh secular priest, the next year a Jesuit, Alfonso Agazzari, was placed in charge of the college; its rectors would remain Jesuits until the Society's suppression in 1773. In 1581 another Jesuit, the Englishman William Good, was appointed the spiritual director. And yet another Jesuit, the Englishman Robert Persons, presumed to proffer advice to the rector, including, 'prepare for us men who will face racks fearlessly.' So the students were not training to be Jesuits but they were receiving in many ways a Jesuit-inspired formation. And the wall paintings, as we shall see, were Jesuit-inspired too.

St Ignatius knew from his own faith journey that the Reformation was not just a doctrinal crisis but also a spiritual one; within the Church many had failed to develop a relationship with God. Catholics, therefore, needed help to come to know Jesus and personally accept him as their Saviour; to use an Ignatian image, to rally to his standard. The Spiritual Exercises were one way the Jesuits achieved this. They had been formulated by Ignatius out of his own spiritual experiences and were a structured programme of mainly imaginative prayer lasting, in their full form, for about a month. But despite St Ignatius' own power of imagination and gift of meditation, the Jesuit Bartolomeo Ricci noted that, 'nevertheless, whenever he was going to meditate on those mysteries of Our Saviour, shortly before his prayer he looked at the pictures that he had collected and displayed around his room for the purpose.' Where imagination faltered in prayer, art could help. So after the final format of the Spiritual Exercises was published in 1548, Ignatius turned to a fellow Jesuit, Jerome Nadal, to devise a work to accompany them which could aid the imagination.

Some have described Jerome Nadal as 'the Second Founder' of the Society. Like Ignatius, he was Spanish, born in 1507 into a prosperous family of the city of Palma on the island of Majorca. Studying in Paris, he met Ignatius, who, with seven others, had bound himself to live in poverty and go to Jerusalem to convert Muslims or, if that failed, to put himself at the service of the pope. Nadal was invited to join this beginning of what would become the Society of Jesus but he declined. Instead, he moved to Avignon, completed a doctorate, was ordained a priest and returned to Spain. Years passed. And then Nadal had an intense spiritual conversion and, reading a circulated letter from India by the Jesuit St Francis Xavier, began to reconsider Ignatius' invitation. In 1545, he travelled to Rome to examine at first hand the new Order. He was impressed yet remained hesitant so Ignatius urged him to make the forty days Spiritual Exercises. During those days Nadal's hesitations disappeared and he decided to join the Society. His conviction that God had brought him to this never wavered and he quickly became one of the most influential members of the Order. In 1548, in Messina, Sicily, he opened the first Jesuit school and from 1554, as Vicar General of the Society, he became an indefatigable visitor of its European houses. A contemporary wrote of Nadal, 'He knows our father, Master Ignatius, well because he has many dealings with him, and he seems to have understood his spirit and comprehended our Institute as well as anyone I know in the Society.' It is said that he influenced more members of the Society than even Ignatius because on each visit to a Jesuit house, Nadal would see all of the Jesuits individually and through him they were connected to the wider Order and its developing vision.

To aid the formation of the Society's novices and students, Nadal had devised for their use illustrated texts of Gospel stories with explanatory captions. After the publication of the Spiritual Exercises, Ignatius asked him to expand these illustrated texts into an annotated and illustrated book of meditations on all the Gospels said at Mass during Easter and on Sundays to help novices, fellow Jesuits or lay people pray imaginatively with the Gospel stories as part of the Exercises or in private prayer. The use of images to collate ideas for the purpose of memorisation had a long tradition. Printing now allowed the mass production of such images, but in this case to enable not memorisation but meditation.

Nadal devised the requested book but it was not published until 1593, sometime after the deaths of both St Ignatius and Nadal. It consisted of 153 illustrated Gospel stories. Each engraving contained a number of scenes, with each scene identified by a capital letter which related to lettered captions of explanation underneath. Nadal's method, however, had been known for some decades and its influence was already apparent in 1558 at the first General Congregation of the Society of Jesus when pictures with explanatory captions for teaching and prayer became part of the Society's policy. The Congregation recommended that the Order's churches and houses should be decorated with didactic wall paintings of stories from scripture or elsewhere, with accompanying texts in Latin and Italian. Yet Nadal's influence did not stop there. At the last session of the Council of Trent in December 1563, which included among its participants two of the original founding members of the Society, the Council Fathers approved the following statement:

> The bishops shall carefully teach this, that by means of the histories of the mysteries of our Redemption, portrayed by paintings or other representations, the people is instructed, and confirmed in (the habit of) remembering, and continually revolving in mind the articles of faith; as also that profit is derived from all sacred images, not only because the people are thereby admonished of the benefits and gifts bestowed upon them by Christ, but also because the miracles which God has performed by means of the saints, and their salutary

examples, are set before the eyes of the faithful; that so they may give God thanks for those things; may order their own lives and manners in imitation of the saints; and may be excited to adore and love God, and to cultivate piety.

Nadal's method, officially encouraged by both the Society and the Council, was soon employed for church decoration. The Jesuit Rector of the German College, Michele Laurentano, like St Philip Neri, promoted the cult of the early Roman martyrs. In his college chapel, he put the martyrs' cult and Nadal's method together, commissioning, in 1581, thirteen wall paintings for the tribune. They depicted the life, suffering and death of the chapel's patron saint, Apollinaris, first Bishop of Ravenna and martyr, and included captions explaining the scenes.

Laurentano had employed the artist Niccolò Circignani. Born around 1530-1535 in Pomarance, sixty miles south-west of Florence, Circignani was known as *Il Pomarancio* after his home town. For many years he worked outside Rome; the contemporary art historian, Vasari, in his Lives of 1568, describes him as a young artist, who had done good work at the Duomo in Orvieto. But by 1580, Circignani was painting frescos in the newly built Tower of the Winds, a two-storey structure rising out of the Vatican Palace, which had been commissioned by Gregory XIII to celebrate his own reform of the calendar (the Gregorian calendar) and to enable further astronomical studies. Circignani's completed frescos are beautiful seascapes; the waves look as if they could tumble out of the wall. Impressed by them, it may have been the pope himself who persuaded the artist to work for the Jesuits, decorating the educational establishments which he had promoted. Circignani's work at the German College was judged a success – unfortunately the chapel, including the frescoes, was destroyed in the mid-1700s – and he became a favourite painter for the Society. They were not interested, however, in swelling seawater but dripping blood.

Circignani's next Jesuit commission can still be visited and admired or, if you are of a squeamish nature, borne: the church of San Stefano Rotondo. Gregory XIII had given it to the new Hungarian College in 1579 but it was not possible to find enough Hungarian students and soon this institute was amalgamated with the German College. San Stefano, amidst the peace and greenery of the Caelian Hill, became a favourite retreat for the college's students on their free day. Today, the church, unusually for Rome, still stands in a quiet spot and on a hot day its interior coolness is a Godsend. Its walls, however, are feverish. In 1582, over five months, Circignani created on those walls 31 pictures with 137 separate incidents. He, principally, painted the figures, leaving the background and accompanying captions to others. Following Laurentano's instructions, within landscapes, early Christian martyr after early Christian martyr of the late Roman Empire, in chronological order and in the greatest detail, is tortured and killed. The paintings are not meant to be works of art in themselves but visual aids for meditation and teaching. Laurentano wrote: 'the sight of an infinite number of torments and martyrdoms moves one to devotion. And even if the painting is mediocre but very devout, many people cannot see it without being moved to tears and spiritually uplifted.' When Pope Sixtus V visited the church a few years later to see the frescos he happily did the hoped-for thing: he burst into tears.

Circignani's next commission in a Jesuit-run house came only a few months later: the English College. This was only possible, however, because of two men, who brought together devotion, knowledge and money.

Chapter 7

GOOD AND GILBERT

William Good was born in 1527 in Glastonbury. The Abbey of Glastonbury was the richest monastery in the land and reputedly the oldest. Yet when Good was twelve years old it was dissolved and the abbot, for opposing the king, was hanged, drawn, and quartered on top of the Tor. His head was placed over the gate to his despoiled and deserted abbey. In 1546, at nineteen years old, Good was admitted to Corpus Christi College, Oxford and became a Fellow two years later. By the time Mary inherited the throne in 1553, Good had spent nearly all of his life in an England turned against the papacy but, following the restoration of Catholicism, he sought ordination to the priesthood. By the end of the queen's reign he was a canon of Wells Cathedral and headmaster of the Grammar School.

Unlike so many others, Good did not turn with the tide at the accession of Elizabeth. By March 1560 he had lost all his ecclesiastical positions and had gone overseas. Two years later, in the Walloon city of Tournai, he was accepted as a novice for the Society of Jesus; the provincial in the Spanish Netherlands had been impressed by his response to the Spiritual Exercises. In 1564 Good was given the relatively dangerous task of helping to establish a university in Ireland. Having narrowly escaped capture in Dublin, he travelled west to Limerick where instead he opened a school. He was rarely left in peace by the Elizabethan authorities but by the late 1560s a school was finally firmly established on the south coast in the walled merchants' town of Youghal. There he developed a reputation as a good preacher. He spent the early 1570s back in the Spanish Netherlands, helping to look after English refugees and leading retreats for them. One refugee, Robert Persons, the future controversialist and great plotter for the Catholic cause, became a

Jesuit because of his retreat with Good. Then, in 1579, Good was sent to Lutheran Sweden. Its king, John III, was theologically aware and attracted to the Catholicism of his first wife. He sought links with Rome and introduced a Communion Service based upon the Roman Missal. But the Swedes were too committed to Lutheranism, too suspicious of Catholicism and, reluctantly, the Jesuits had to accept that nothing substantial would happen. So Good left and went to Rome, where this now much-travelled Canon of Wells was appointed Spiritual Director of the English College. William Allen wrote: 'In that Reverend Father Good, a man that is good indeed, is to be confessor of the college, I greatly rejoice; for he is especially qualified to form character and skilled in the whole art of direction.'

Good's talents, however, went further and included history and controversy. For when it was decided, in a manner we do not know exactly how, to commission Circignani to paint, as at the German College and San Stefano, a series of wall paintings at the English College, it was Good who organised the project and devised the subject matter of the paintings. But it was someone else who raised the money and injected youthful passion.

Edward Dering was an outspoken Puritan clergyman in the Church of England. He was clear that under Elizabeth, the country's reformed church still had vestiges of papacy and that the people were not being properly instructed in the faith. In fact, when he was given the opportunity to preach in the queen's presence, he told her what he thought:

> And yet you in the meanwhile that all these whoredoms are committed, you at whose hands God will require it, you sit still and are careless, let men do as they list. It touch not belike your common wealth, and therefore you are so well contented to let all alone.

No Elizabethan sermon was more often reprinted and one young man who returned repeatedly to listen to Dering was George Gilbert. Born in Suffolk and educated in London and Cambridge, his family were wealthy and, at an early age, he inherited extensive landed estates. He loved the martial arts, giving much time to riding, vaulting and fencing. In 1580, when he was about twenty-eight years old, a Government informer described him as 'bending somewhat in the knees, fair-complexioned, reasonably well-coloured, little hair on his face, and short if he have any, thick somewhat of speech.' In the late 1570s our young Puritan received royal permission to go overseas and he made his way to Paris, where he cut a dashing figure at the king's court. In the French capital he met a fellow Englishman and Catholic Jesuit priest, Thomas Darbyshire. They talked on spiritual matters and, under the influence of Darbyshire, Gilbert's Calvinism waned. He decided to travel to Rome and there met the Jesuit, Robert Persons, who, in 1579, received him into the Church and acted as his Confirmation sponsor. From that time, Gilbert embraced a life of heroic spirituality. He maintained his martial pursuits but added to them much prayer and fasting.

Gilbert soon returned to London and formed around himself the Catholic Association: like-minded and equally wealthy young Englishmen, ready to devote themselves 'to the common support of Catholics'. Their energies became focused with the advent of a new mission from Rome led by Robert Persons, disguised as an army captain, and his fellow English Jesuit, Edmund Campion, who pretended to be a jewel merchant. The Jesuits hoped to encourage Catholics, prevent their absorption into the state church and establish a network of support. On their arrival in London, Gilbert, with the support of the Association, hid them and, for the rest of their time in England, generously financed their activities and provided their everyday needs. When Persons left London in early July and set out on a missionary tour to the Midlands and the West Country, Gilbert accompanied him. A couple of years later, Gilbert wrote an essay entitled *A way to deal with persons of all sorts so as to convert them and bring them back to a better way of life – based on the system and methods used by Fr Robert Persons and Fr Edmund Campion.* Within it he described the qualities necessary in a gentleman to support the work of the missionary priests:

> As soon as any father or learned priest has entered an heretical country he should seek out some gentleman to be his companion. This man should be zealous, loyal, discreet and determined to help him in this service of God, and should be able to undertake honourably the expenses of both of them. He should have a first-rate reputation as a good comrade and as being knowledgeable about the country, the roads and paths, the habits and disposition of the gentry and people of the place, and should be a man who has many relations and friends and much local information.

Persons and Gilbert spent the next few months in disguise, travelling the country and meeting secretly at houses where Catholics would gather for

Confession, Mass and words of priestly encouragement. Gilbert poured his money, energy and wit into supporting this venture. By November they were back in London setting up a secret printing press on what, hundreds of years later, would become the site of West Ham United's football ground. In the spring of 1581, Persons became increasingly concerned for Gilbert's safety; his wealth and Catholicism made him too well known. The Government had already seized some of his estate for his nonconformity; it would only be a matter of time before he was arrested. So forcefully persuaded by Persons, Gilbert left England in May. In July Campion was arrested and Persons himself fled to the continent. Neither Gilbert nor Persons would ever return.

Gilbert, at first, went to the English College at Rheims. Its rector, William Allen, because of Gilbert's financial generosity, later described him as 'patrum presbyterorum patronus' ('the greatest patron of the Catholic clergy'). He then travelled to Rome and settled as a pensioner at the English College but his hope was to return to England and, if necessary, be martyred. He would say to students that he wished not to die in a soft bed but after having been stretched many times on a rack, and then torn and ripped up by executioners. A few years later, in October 1583, the rector, Agazzari, wrote a long letter to the General of the Society of Jesus about Gilbert. It described his life and manner at the college and it is clear that the rector thought him a saint. According to Agazzari, when Gilbert was not busy championing the needs of England with the Princes of the Church, he devoted himself to prayer and study and his particular delight was to meditate upon the martyrs. Agazzari wrote: 'His devotion towards the saints led him to visit their churches very frequently, hence he never let a fortnight pass without making the usual round of the seven basilicas, visiting each one with great devotion, generally alone, and when fewer would be there, that he might better preserve recollection.' Gilbert's love for England's contemporary martyrs was no less. Edmund Campion, Ralph Sherwin – the first student of the College – and Alexander Briant of the English College in Rheims had died together at Tyburn's gallows on 1 December 1581. While recommending their example to fellow students and praising martyrdom in general, Agazzari records that Gilbert spoke of:

> . . . the consolation which God communicates to those who think of the multitude of delights, and the shortness of the sufferings, the greatness of the

glory, and the slightness of the ignominy which is to be borne. He exhorted them to meditate upon the desires of the saints to die for Christ, and how eager they were to be found in similar circumstances to the present students of the English College. To this end he suggested means of cultivating in themselves the desire of so blessed a crown; one of which was to meditate often on the Passion of our Lord.

It is not surprising that, with men such as Gilbert in residence, the English College should want to celebrate the Church's newest martyrs in England. Agazzari recorded Gilbert's role in the creation of the wall paintings:

> The holy youth took great pains to learn the names of all the English martyrs of former and modern times, and caused their acts of martyrdom to be represented in paintings, with which he adorned the whole church of this college in the way that your Paternity [the General of the Society] has seen. This cost him seven hundred scudi, having collected for the purpose contributions from several of his English friends. He used to say that his object in this was not only to honour those glorious martyrs, and to manifest before the world the glory and splendour of the Church in England, but also that the students and the college, beholding the example of their predecessors, might stimulate themselves to follow it; moreover that Rome and the world, when seeing the deplorable state of the country, might be moved to pray for it.

So although it was Good who devised and commissioned the wall paintings, Gilbert's financial support and youthful passion were essential.

Chapter 8

PAINTED MARTYRS

In late 1582 or early 1583, Circignani began painting in the church at the English College. He followed the same layout of annotated scenes as at San Apollinare and San Stefano. The wall paintings consist of thirty-four pictures, which can be divided into two separate but continuous groups. The first twenty-four pictures, with their focus upon martyrs and missionaries, cover England's history from around the year 63 to the late Middle Ages. The second group of ten pictures begins with the martyrdom of Fisher and More in 1535 and ends with the execution of Richard Thirkeld at York on 29 May 1583. The College must have heard of his martyrdom as Circignani was painting. The artist at the end, therefore, was not so much creating a historical record as a newsreel. The paintings are undeniably gory; they do not conceal the reality of violence but then nor did sixteenth-century life. In the 1580s, the English College adjoined the Corte Savella Prison (later generations of students would complain of the inmates' groans) and public executions were carried out around the corner in the Campo de' Fiori. Life was physically tough; pain was casually inflicted.

For seven chapters we have considered the pre-history of, and the influences upon, the wall paintings. Now it is time to conclude, as definitively as we dare, what are their purposes.

Jesuit Practice

Since the Jesuits were committed to decorating their chapels in a didactic manner, it is natural that the English College, though not a Jesuit house, should be influenced by its Jesuit staff and copy the work of other institutions guided by the Society. The only difference for the English College was the subject matter. William Good devised a scheme which reflected the particular concerns of the English and Welsh Catholic community.

Celebration

The English College was well known in Rome, visited by pilgrims, Princes of the Church and people of influence. As in the days of the hospice, when its governors had placed an inscription above its door proclaiming to Rome and the world that France was rightly England's, so now, despite the country's self-enforced Reformation isolation, the college commissioned the wall paintings to remind its visitors, as well as its students, of England and Wales' glorious history and saints. The paintings also celebrate that the Church in England and Wales had been no less blessed with martyrs in the early days than Rome but now, in the present days, surpassed the Eternal City.

Do not forget

The paintings also kept the plight of England and Wales before the eyes of the world. In 1582, Gregory XIII published a bull *Omnipotens Deus*, commending the needs of English Catholics to the rest of Catholic Europe. He described the 'unheard-of cruelty suffered by the Catholics in England, and how a great many of them are forced to leave the country in order not to lose their faith, and many others in that country undergo intense torture ending in death.' In association with the bull, the Jesuit General sent out a letter to the Jesuit Provincials, pointing out that England was the only country in which Catholics were persecuted by both the imposition of heretical beliefs and by penalties for not attending Protestant services. A year after that papal bull and the general's letter, anyone could walk into the English College and see for themselves those 'unheard-of' cruelties and persecutions. And these images demanded action from the viewer: prayers for England and Wales' conversion, financial support for the students and Catholic exiles and, perhaps, plans to overthrow Elizabeth.

Prayer

At San Stefano, the students of the German College would process around the church, praying before the pictures of the early martyrs, which formed a litany of the saints. There is no evidence of such a practice at the English College; the church did not have an ambulatory as at San Stefano. The paintings, however, must have shaped the prayers of the students and the celebration of Mass. Every day the students listened to an excerpt from the martyrology about the particular saints of that day. Then when they entered their church they saw a national martyrology in paint. Remembering that according to Catholic teaching the Church on earth is joined at Mass with the Communion of Saints – the Church in heaven – the students' prayers must have been coloured and inspired by the images of those saints, including fellow students, seen by the flickering light of candles.

Encouragement

In December 1563, the Council of Trent taught that the saints are to be seen as 'salutary examples' and that they should be 'set before the eyes of the faithful, so that they may give God thanks for those things, may fashion their own life and conduct in imitation of the saints and be moved to adore and love God and cultivate piety.' The wall paintings were not just decoration. They grimly taught the students what they would face in England but, more importantly, they encouraged them with the examples of the virtue and courage of those who had gone before. Martyrdom is part of English and Welsh history, the wall paintings taught the students, and it may also be your privilege to earn a martyr's crown. As William Allen wrote, 'where God gives the grace of martyrdom, it is a joyful sign of mercy and that he will not forsake the place or people, which he blesses with so high and rare a benediction.' And we must not forget how powerful, how moving, it must have been for the students that the last scenes of the wall paintings depicted not long-dead saints but fellows who had only just left college and prayed in that church. Ludovico Jacobilli, a seventeenth-century Italian from Umbria, commented, in his book on Umbrian saints, that we learn from the saints how to behave, particularly when they are local to us: 'So much more easily (can we follow them) owing to the fact that the authors of these actions were made of the same stuff as us, from the same region and province and flourished in sanctity at every age and in every century and that, furthermore, they unceasingly help us in Heaven with their prayers and intercessions.' Perhaps this was a common theme of sermons in the college church with the preacher gesturing towards the walls.

A response to Bale

'[The book] has done more hurt alone to simple souls in our country by infecting and poisoning them unawares under the bait of pleasant histories, fair pictures, and painted pageants, than many other of the most pestilent books together.' This is Robert Persons' complaint against Foxe's *Acts and Monuments*. Not only did Foxe describe in great detail the deaths of his Protestant martyrs, he included many engravings to fire the imagination. Catholics, however, did not just complain; they responded in kind. In 1582, Allen sent to Agazzari a book he had written about the recent martyrdoms of fifteen secular priests and the Jesuit Campion. Allen wanted it translated into good Latin style. He said of the book's account that, 'You will see in it a constancy quite equal to that of the ancient martyrs.' The book was not translated into Latin but into Italian by 'someone at the English College' and was published the next year in 1583. It included six engravings of martyrdoms, which may have been originally created for a work of a similar nature by Persons, published in 1582: *An Epistle of the Persecution of Catholicks in Englande*. Persons had said that he was writing of Catholic martyrs as a response to tales of Protestant ones. Circignani's own depictions of Campion's torture and death are clearly inspired by the illustrations in Allen's book. So even before the creation of the wall paintings at the English College, the exiled Catholic community was already responding to illustrated Protestant depictions of martyrdom with its own published illustrations of Catholic martyrs. Yet the wall paintings go further. They are a detailed response to John Bale.

In his 1547 work, *The latter examinacyon of Anne Askew, with the elucydacyon of J Bale*, Bale had elaborated his own version of the history of the English Church. As in his other work, already outlined, Bale repeated his argument that the Church in England was first founded, without any involvement from Rome, by Joseph of Arimathea and then built up by King Lucius. The invading pagan Saxons, however, pushed the Christian Britons westward. Next, according to Bale, St Augustine, the minion of the Antichrist, converted the Saxons to a corrupt form of

Christianity. They then persecuted the true Church among the Britons. Every martyr of the post-Augustine mission was dismissed by Bale as a creature of the Antichrist and the miracles associated with them were ridiculed. This version of history, which denied the Catholic Church any links with the origins of the Church in England and Wales, enabled Bale to portray the Reformation not as a break with the past, but as a rediscovery of the original and true British Church. Foxe stuck to this line in *Acts and Monuments*.

In response to Bale, twenty-seven pictures of the English College's wall paintings depict martyrs which the former Carmelite had dismissed. By simply portraying them and emphasising their miracles, either through depiction or in the accompanying annotating texts, Good defended these martyrs and their validating miracles and so, most importantly, the Catholic origins of the Church in England and Wales. The wall paintings share Thomas Stapleton's reason for translating Bede: present the history of the Church in England as it really was and you will disprove Bale. It is striking that from the twenty-fifth picture, which includes St Thomas More, there are no miracles. This is no oversight. Miracles are granted to missionaries and martyrs when planting the Church among pagans. St Thomas More and the others, however, had died for papal authority and Church unity in a land where Rome had already established the Church. The lack of miracles in their period, therefore, is proof in itself that the true Church is already established and does not need to be, nor can be, built up by the reformers. Good dismisses Foxe's account of Protestant miracles by the absence of Catholic ones. The most important function, therefore, of the wall paintings was to let the witness of the martyrs show that from its beginnings the Church in England and Wales was part of the universal Church whose head, St Peter, and his successors, have received their authority from Christ. Bale had destroyed the notion of the continuity of the Catholic Church in England and Wales. The wall paintings of the English College restored it.

Didactic

Allen had made Bede's *History* a set text for his seminarians so that 'they may be able to show our countrymen from it that our nation did not receive in the beginning any other than the Catholic faith which we profess and was converted to no other of Christianity except that which we preach to them, and that their forefathers bore the name of Christians and were such only as members of this Catholic Christendom.'

In 1581 Edmund Campion had requested the opportunity for a fair debate on the central issues of religion. He was never given the chance before his martyrdom but future generations might be. The wall paintings were part of the students' preparation for that chance. Each scene builds up an historical argument to counter Bale's version of England's history. They fulfil Allen's purpose in having students read Bede. They were to enable them to win back souls on the mission by helping them to question the foundations of the new religion; as the Marian Bishop Hopton used to enquire of Protestants: 'Do you not believe as your father did? Was he not an honest man?'

George Gilbert was given hardly any time to enjoy the finished paintings. At the beginning of October 1583, a few months after their completion and just as he was about to set off to France on a diplomatic mission on behalf of the pope, he fell ill with a fever. Agazzari has left us a moving account of his final hours at the English College on 6 October. It includes this description:

> I then presented to him that little crucifix which the martyr Alexander Briant made, and carried with him to the place of execution. Mr Gilbert on seeing it, took it with the greatest affection and kissed it, then lifting up his eyes to heaven he called to his assistance those three first most glorious martyrs, Campion, Sherwin and Briant, exclaiming, "O my Lord, why have I not been found worthy of those ropes, of those racks, of the most precious deaths of those my sweet and dear companions? Why have I not been myself for Thy love cut into pieces and lacerated? O ropes, O racks, O knives, O death most desirable. Who will grant me now that in some part of London I may be treated by you as you did treat my dear Father Campion, and that you may be the means of bringing me to my Saviour as you brought him?"

Gilbert died a few hours later. He was probably only thirty-one years old.

The wall paintings themselves were ultimately no more durable. By the end of the eighteenth century, the English College church had badly deteriorated and was no longer in use. In 1798 the college was forced to close for twenty years because of the Napoleonic wars. After the college was re-opened, the church and the paintings clinging to its walls were knocked down and eventually, in the 1860s, a new church was built. However, a book of the wall paintings with a complete set of prints by J B de Cavalleriis had been published in 1584 by the college. The work was entitled *Ecclesiae Anglicanae Trophaea* (*The Trophies of the English Church*) and enabled the wall paintings to have a much wider audience. Throughout Europe, men and women were able to admire England and Wales' glorious Catholic past and marvel at the sacrifices of her present Catholic people. In 1883 the artist Silverio Capparoni recreated from Cavalleriis' engravings the lost paintings on the walls of the tribune of the new college church. No longer were the students surrounded by them at Mass, but at least they could visit them above when mindful to do so. It is time for us to visit them, one by one.

THE PICTURES

A | S. Petrus Apostolus Angliam ingressus multos ad Christum convertit . Tem
pla construit . Sacerdotes . et episcopos ordinat .
B | S. Joseph ab Aramathea ut in Anglia cum 12. Sociis habitare possit ab
Arvirago Rege impetrat : Ubi plurimos Christo fide
et baptismo adiungit .
C | S. Simon Apostolus in Anglia Evangelium praedicat . multos illi credet̄ es baptizat .

PICTURE I

A.   St Peter the Apostle, coming to England, converts many people to Christ. He builds churches. He ordains priests and bishops.

The first picture is dominated by St Peter. This does not seem right. William Blake's poem Jerusalem has kept alive the story that Jesus visited England as a boy with his 'uncle', Joseph of Arimathea. The legend of Joseph's later visit in this land is still known. But to say that St Peter had come to England surely means that William Good had become a myth-maker like John Bale. In *De Unitate*, Pole had given scriptural reasons, supported and developed by Tradition, for the divinely ordained role of the pope. For Catholics the argument over which missionaries first converted England is a red herring. In the earliest days of the Church, when there was no major division, to have been baptized by any Christian missionary would have been understood as membership of the Catholic Church and unity with the bishop of Rome. But, of course, these paintings are part of the battle over historical continuity – however really necessary or productive that battle was – and what could better trump Bale's supposedly autonomous Church founded by Joseph of Arimathea from Jerusalem than St Peter himself bringing the Faith to England from Rome?

Thomas Stapleton had already written of St Peter's mission to England in *A fortresse*, his appendix to his translation of Bede, and William Good had some grounds for accepting this idea. An anonymous tenth-century Greek commentary on St Peter and St Paul, attributed to Simeon Metaphrastes, a Byzantine hagiographer, and based, perhaps, upon an earlier Greek menology (a book of lives of the saints for liturgical use) of the sixth century, claimed that St Peter spent twenty-three years at Rome, in Western Europe, and in particular that he lived in Britain, where he converted many people, founded many churches, and ordained bishops, priests and deacons. Except for no reference to deacons, this is exactly what Good states in this scene. Cesare Baronius, the great ecclesiastical historian and cardinal, would be highly critical of this document, pointing out, for example, that its citations from the fourth-century historian Eusebius are not real. This criticism, however, was not published until a few years after Good's death in Naples in 1586. Good had acted, if a little hopefully, at least in good faith. So St Peter is painted holding the traditional keys of his authority and ordaining men while, in the mountainous background, the churches he has founded rise up beneath the English sky.

B.   St Joseph of Arimathea asks King Arviragus for leave to live in England with twelve companions: and there he brings many to Christ by means of faith and baptism.

Glastonbury is a place of faith, myth and martyrdom. Its abbey was probably the oldest and richest in England, originally dating from the early seventh century. Around 1130, William of Malmesbury, the chief English historian of his generation, stayed there and researched its archives. In his work, *On the Antiquity of Glastonbury*, he recorded the community's belief that Glastonbury was the site of the first and oldest church in England, having been built in the first century by missionaries from Gaul sent by the Apostle St Philip. The evidence for this was a charter, which included a history of Glastonbury, supposedly dating from the time of St Patrick – the alleged first abbot of the monastery – which William had found in the archives. He was, however, clearly suspicious of this document's worth and despite including its allegations, he was happier to write of King Lucius, whose request to Pope Eleutherius led, in an alternative tradition, to the first church at Glastonbury.

William's original manuscript was not left unaltered. By 1250, at the latest, members of the abbey had dramatically developed his original and cautious account to include a new figure: Joseph of Arimathea. According to the altered account, in 63 AD St Philip sent twelve missionaries, led by Joseph, to England. Having asked King Arviragus's leave to evangelize, they built their first church at Glastonbury. In Geoffrey of Monmouth's *The History of the Kings of Britain*, Arviragus, the son of Cymbeline, was the king of Britain at the time. This was a nice touch of embellishment by our monkish forger – linking a myth with a supposed historical character. Geoffrey's *History*, however, which traces the story of Britain from its purported foundation by Brutus, the great-grandson of the Trojan Aeneas, to the last British King, Cadwallader, who eventually abandoned the country to the invading Saxons, with many tales of Arthur and Merlin in between, is almost a complete fiction. The last addition to the legend of Joseph and Glastonbury comes from the pen of the monk, John of Glastonbury, who wrote at the beginning of the fifteenth century. He tells us that Joseph brought with him the Holy Grail – not the cup from the Last Supper as is widely presumed – but two cruets, stoppered vessels resembling tall, slender jugs, the one containing blood from Christ, the other water, which Joseph had collected from Christ as he died upon the cross. These were buried, according to John, with Joseph in Glastonbury. In the painting, therefore, Joseph, wearing a pilgrim's purse as befits this wanderer, is shown addressing King Arviragus, while holding one of the cruets; a companion holds the other. In the background you can see Joseph's fellow missionaries with, perhaps, that very first church in Glastonbury, and in England, behind them.

We could be embarrassed by the inclusion of this evolved story but it was taken seriously at the time. Glastonbury Abbey was able to argue that it was the principal monastery of the land because of its 'chronicled' antiquity. A John Blome in 1345 sought permission from the chancery of Edward III to excavate for Joseph's body in the land around the abbey. He received permission. At international Church Councils the precedence of the 'nations' was determined by the date of a country's conversion; beginning with the Council of Pisa in 1409, the English Crown argued that Joseph's mission gave England precedence before all. And John Bale, as we have seen, used the legend to invent a distinct British Church, free from the corruption of the papacy.

Good included Joseph of Arimathea because the saint was a proud part of England's story; part of her beginning. Joseph's mission could only undermine the English Church's links with Rome if you believed that it was possible to have a Church without Peter; but for any orthodox Catholic it was not. Good was also probably confident about the cumulative effect of the evidence he was presenting. And he was himself born in Glastonbury, receiving his early education at 'the hospice of Joseph of Arimathea for gentlemen' and, as a boy of eight, he served Mass in the chapel dedicated to St Joseph. Good has left us an account of his childhood, which includes this memory:

> At Glastonbury there were bronze plates as a perpetual memorial, chapels, crypts, crosses, arms, the keeping of the feast (of Joseph) on 27 July, as long as the monks enjoyed the protection of kings by their charters. Now all these things have perished in the ruins. The monks never knew for certain the place of this saint's burial, or pointed it out. They said . . . that when his body should be found, the whole world should wend their way thither on account of the number and wondrous nature of the miracles worked there.
>
> Amongst other things, I remember to have seen at Glastonbury on a stone cross, overthrown during this queen's reign (Elizabeth I), a bronze plate, on which was carved an inscription relating that Joseph of Arimathea came to Britain thirty years after Christ's Passion, with eleven or twelve companions: that he was allowed by Arviragus the king to dwell at Glastonbury, which was then an island called Avalon, in a simple and solitary life: and that he brought with him two small vessels in which was some of the most holy blood and water which had flowed from the side of the dead Christ.

For Good, Joseph was not just a part of Britain's history; he was family. The abbey of Glastonbury was dissolved by King Henry in 1539. Its last abbot is included in the twenty-seventh picture of the wall paintings. He was hanged, drawn, and quartered for opposing the king.

C.   St Simon the Apostle preaches the Gospel in England. He baptizes many who believe in it.

St Simon the Apostle's presence in England may seem as surprising as St Peter's. He disappears from historical record after Pentecost but the most enduring legend from before the sixth century has him martyred with St Jude in Persia. There is, however, another account which dates from the sixth century and is alleged to have been drawn up by St Dorotheus, an ascetical writer, who founded a monastery at Gaza around 540. It states, 'Simon the Zealot having passed through all Mauritania, and the region of the Africans, and preached Christ, was afterwards crucified by them in Britain, and being made perfect by martyrdom, was there buried.' This account passed into many Greek menologies. For Bale, St Simon's mission, like St Joseph's, was another founding moment of the Church in England; another mission from the East with no connection to Rome. Good was happy to include St Simon because he had already trumped Bale with St Peter. And, altogether, he must have been filled with patriotic pride at the thought of England's claim upon these three saints. In the international city of Rome, at the heart of the Church, Good celebrated in paint the apostolic and antique claims of the Church in England.

So myth, as well as history, was fought over, and in 1583 the battle was still as fresh as the paint. William Fulke, the Vicar of Great Warley, Essex, was the eminent defender of the reformed Church of England during the 1570s and 1580s in the face of Catholic criticism. In a work of 1584, he cited both St Joseph's and St Simon's missions to England as evidence of a local church autonomous from Rome and free of her perversities. The paint dried, but not people's appetite for historical controversy.

A | S. Lucius Angliae Rex a Fugatio, et Damiano, S. Eleutherii P.P. legatis baptizatur, einsque regnū tunc primum publice fidem Christi recepit.

B | Idem regno composito Evangelium praedicaturus in Germaniam se confert.
Ubi post lapidationem, Churiae Episcopus cum esset, a plebe infideli perimitur.

C | S. Emerita S. Lucii Soror Tremontii pro Christo igne crematur.

PICTURE II

A.   St Lucius, king of England, is baptized by Fugatius and Damian, legates of Pope St Eleutherius, and his kingdom then, for the first time, publicly receives the faith of Christ.

B.   Having settled his kingdom, he sets out for Germany to preach the faith there. He became the bishop of Chur, and was stoned to death by an unbelieving mob.

C.   St Emerita, sister of St Lucius, is burned at Tremontium for the Christian faith.

We know only a little about the history of Christianity in England before St Augustine of Canterbury's mission. The earlier we go, the less we know. We may know something, however, from the second century. The earliest part of the *Liber Pontificalis* (a collection of early papal biographies), compiled about 530, has this entry in the biography of the thirteenth pope, St Eleutherius (c. 175-c. 189):

> He received a letter from Lucius, a British king, to the effect that he might be made a Christian by his order.

St Bede includes this event in his *History*, with some additions to the bald statement:

> In the year of our Lord 156 Marcus Antoninus Verus was made emperor together with his brother Aurelius Commodus. He was the fourteenth after Augustus. In their time, while a holy man called Eleutherius was bishop of the church at Rome, Lucius, a king of Britain, sent him a letter praying that he might be made a Christian by a rescript from him. His pious request was quickly granted and the Britons preserved the faith which they had received, inviolate and entire, in peace and quiet, until the time of the Emperor Diocletian.

Lucius' story is later developed and embellished, particularly by Geoffrey of Monmouth, who refers to him a number of times in his *History of the Kings of Britain*. According to him, after Lucius' baptism, which the king had requested because of tales of miracles by Christian missionaries, the first dioceses were founded. The bishops' seats were purposefully placed where druids once ruled. An editor of William of Malmesbury's *On the Antiquity of Glastonbury* is the first to number or name the missionaries from Pope Eleutherius: Faganus and Duvianus. Their names will change through the centuries. If it is not too tedious to note, the first documentary evidence for the names Fugatius and Damian, which William Good uses in the painting, is from John Leland's *De Rebus Britannicus Collectanea*. He records that he found them in the *Annals of the Church of Rochester* (*c.* 1224).

But enough of this, especially as nearly every scholar now doubts Lucius' existence (Cardinal Baronius had already begun to question the account in the late sixteenth century – the alleged dates of the king did not work). At the beginning of the twentieth century it was argued, to the satisfaction of most, that the statement in the *Liber Pontificalis* had been transcribed incorrectly and that it originally referred to Agbar IX – also named Lucius – King of Edessa in northern Mesopotamia, who was perhaps converted after sending enquiries to the pope. The *Liber Pontificalis* had been our only real evidence for Lucius; with that gone, Lucius goes.

King Lucius, however, remains important to us because in the sixteenth century, he was fought over by Protestants and Catholics. As we have seen, Bale tweaked Bede's account of the king's conversion, minimising Lucius' request to the pope. But surprisingly, he ignored a remarkable discovery in the late-1520s in London's Guildhall, among manuscripts recording laws from the reign of King Edward the Confessor: a letter from Pope Eleutherius to King Lucius. It was found by one of Henry VIII's researchers and was included in the *Collectanea Satis Copiosa* (1530), which brought together diverse material supporting Henry's increasingly strident claim that as king of England he had no spiritual superior on earth. The letter was supposedly a papal response to Lucius' request for knowledge of the Roman legal system. In it the pope describes the king, magically for Henry, as 'God's vicar in your kingdom'. We now know, however, that the letter dates from the reign of King John. It ends with the papal warning that if the king does not uphold the Law, he shall lose his realm. Perhaps, William Hardel, the Mayor of London and a signatory to the *Magna Carta*, forged himself a little Petrine help for the barons' dealings with the king. After Henry VIII broke away from Rome the letter was once again forgotten. King

Lucius' importance, however, was not.

In November 1554, Pole, as we have seen, during his speech to Parliament before the reconciliation of England to Rome, makes much of Lucius. Britons, he poetically claimed, were the first of all people to receive the Gospel 'from the Apostolyke sea universallye, and not in partes as other countreyes, nor by one and one, as clockes increase theyre howres by distinction of tymes but altogether at once, as it were in a moment.' He emphasised the providence of this, God's work in this: England's prosperity began with her turning to Rome. The importance of Lucius for Catholic apologists is evident in William Good's allocation of a whole scene to him. In 1559, as Elizabeth attacked the established Catholic Church, bishops and senior clergy followed Pole's novel lead of turning to Lucius. John Feckenham, Abbot of Westminster, speaking in the House of Lords, denounced his opponents' changeability. The religion of the Prayer Book, he said, was scarcely two years old, while Catholicism had been established by papal mission in England for one thousand and four hundred years from the days of King Lucius and this 'auncyent religion and manner of servinge of God . . . is the very true and perfect religion and of God.' Nicholas Heath, the Archbishop of York, who had supported Henry and Edward's religious reforms, now took his stand with the pope and King Lucius. The Gospel, he reminded the Lords, had come to England in three plantings – that of Pope Eleutherius at Lucius' request, that of St Augustine and, most recently, that of Cardinal Pole – all from Rome. If Rome was the creature that she was now being described as by Protestants, how is it that the Gospel had been planted so well? Heath finished his own amazing personal journey by declaring that the unity of the Church was founded on Peter's authority, and therefore 'by our leaping out of Peter's shippe, we must nedes be overwhelmed by the waters of schism, sects and division.'

For the exiled Catholic apologists of Elizabeth's reign, Lucius would remain an important piece of evidence: this first complete conversion of the country, it was thought, had been directly achieved by a mission from Rome, requested by a king who had submitted to the pope's authority. Having ignored Lucius since the 'divorce' proceedings, except for Bale's tweaking, apologists for the Church of England now began to lob him back at their Catholic opponents. John Jewel, to whose 'challenge' sermon Stapleton had replied, adopted two positions on Lucius in his *Defence of the Apology* (1567), which became standard among the reformers. First, Britain had not been converted by papal mission: Joseph of Arimathea had already brought the Gospel to England; the Christian community that he began must have told Lucius about Christ. Second, Jewel quoted the 'letter' from Pope Eleutherius: England had no need of the pope, for the Crown had the necessary spiritual authority. Archbishop Parker of Canterbury, keen to assure doubters of the historicity of the Church of England, turned to Lucius in his 1568 Preface to the Bishops' Bible, the authorised translation of the scriptures until the King James version. Parker wrote that 'being in great love with the true faith' Lucius asked for advice from Rome and was sent in return the 'letter'. The mission itself, according to the archbishop, was dominated by Elvanus and Meduinus, the two messengers whom Lucius had sent to Rome. They are first added to the story around 1125 in its telling by the old *Book of Llandaff*. It is these two, missionaries to their own land, not any men of the pope, who, on returning with the letter, spread the Gospel: 'for the eloquence and knowledge they had in the holy Scriptures, repaired home again to King Lucius, and by their holy preachings, Lucius, and the noble men of the whole of Britaine, received their baptism.' Finally, just as one last example, Sergeant Wray – who would later preside at the trial of St Edmund Campion – became the new speaker of the Commons in 1571 and in his opening speech to the House, reminded them of the obedience they owed to the Crown, which had both temporal and spiritual authority in the realm since the reign of King Lucius, who could make 'lawes by his own good discretion, for that hee was the vicar of Christ over the people of Brittane.'

In the English College painting, however, Lucius' request to the pope and his baptism are not the most prominent details, despite the crucial nature of the issue. Rather it is Lucius' supposed martyrdom in Switzerland which takes central stage. According to Geoffrey of Monmouth, Lucius died and was buried in Gloucester. This is supported by a plaque at St Peter-upon-Cornhill, which is built upon the highest point in the City of London and is, according to a late medieval legend, the site of the first church in London, founded by Lucius himself. Yet there is a continental eighth-century work, *Vita Lucii Confessoris Curiensis*, which states that Lucius, King of Britain, left his home and travelled to Germany as a missionary and eventually became Bishop of Chur where he was martyred for the faith. Chur, the capital of the Swiss Canton Graubünden, and the seat of the local bishop, still honours this British king. The Swiss connection was known in England by the sixteenth century. Foxe dismissed it out of hand, referring to Lucius' death 'in his own land, and burial at Gloucester.'

The third event of the scene is the martyrdom of St Emerita, sister of Lucius. Her name and existence are unknown until 896 when she first appears in a martyrology probably composed by Blessed Notker of St Gall. Her memory is still venerated at the village of Trimmis, three miles from Chur.

The principal actors in the first scene of this painting are the papal missionaries, Fugatius and Damian. After the apostolic missions of St Peter, St Joseph and St Simon, which converted only a few, Lucius initiates a mission for complete public conversion. It is, however, Good emphasises, the pope's legates who achieve this and Lucius, by requesting and receiving baptism at their hands, acknowledges the pope as head of the Church. Good then places Lucius of Chur rather than Lucius of Britain at the centre of the scene. Bale had dismissed many of the martyrs of the Anglo-Saxon Church because of their link to St Augustine's mission and because they had travelled as missionaries from England to other Saxon nations. He was trying to create a history of England with no association to a missionary movement because this would break another historical link with the international papal Church. But the English Jesuit, Robert Persons, in his 1603 work, *Treatise of three conversions*, wrote that the English Church had obeyed a divine injunction:

> After our conversion, in forraine countreys, stirring up holy men of great zeale in England to go abroade into other kingdoms, to preach his word unto the gentiles, and to seeke martyrdome there, seeing it was not to be had for the present at home.

In his depiction of Lucius, therefore, Good is reminding his audience that from the earliest days England has provided martyrs for the faith and, as importantly, missionaries, including martyred missionaries. When we reach the days of the Saxon missionaries, Good will eagerly display their spilt blood. Lucius of Chur was, in fact, a new and powerful addition to the debate with Protestants because Chur in this period, as today, was the seat of a Catholic bishop 'established' by Lucius and so, whatever Protestants may try to argue, Lucius' creed included the Petrine Office because that is what he planted in Chur. Therefore, Good was arguing, from its earliest days the Church in England has been part of the universal Catholic Church, not an insular creature of the Crown.

A	S. Albanus, ponte turba completo, flumen sicco pede transit.
B	Idem capite plectitur, quod complexus miles, cui ossa pro Christo contusa fuerant, sanatur.
C	Is miles, capite amputato, in sanguine suo baptizatur.
D	S. Julius, S. Aaron, aliique complures pro fide obtruncatur.

PICTURE III

A.   St Alban, when a crowd blocks the bridge, crosses the river dry-shod.

B.   St Alban is beheaded, and a soldier whose bones had been broken for Christ, embraces his head, and is healed.

C.   The same soldier is beheaded, and baptized in his own blood.

This picture celebrates England's proto-martyr, St Alban. Bede tells us that the martyrdom happened outside Verulamium, which is now St Albans; the mountains that rise behind the city, however, do not necessarily make you think of Hertfordshire. Circignani presents St Alban's last moments. What brought him to this hillside and execution was a general persecution of Christians, during which he hid a priest in his house in the city. The pagan Alban is impressed by the priest's prayers and vigils and, by divine grace, comes to faith in Christ. When soldiers appear, looking for the priest, Alban puts on the cleric's cloak and pretends to be him. Brought before the judge, this subterfuge is discovered but Alban refuses to sacrifice to the gods, saying only: 'I shall ever adore and worship the true and living God who created all things.' He is then led out to be executed and the painting describes the rest: the place of execution is on the other side of the river from the city but the bridge is full of people coming to watch, preventing Alban crossing it himself; and thus he prays for the river to stop and crosses its dry bed. After his beheading, a soldier who had been earlier beaten for his own Christian faith, holds St Alban's head and is healed of his injuries; this soldier is then beheaded and baptized in his own blood. It is interesting to note that Good has presented different details from Bede, at least concerning the soldier who is martyred. In Bede it is the original executioner, who having refused to kill St Alban, is beheaded after him. There is no reference to his first being beaten or holding the proto-martyr's head.

Bede states that Alban was martyred in 301, during Diocletian's persecution. However, an earlier account of the martyrdom, which was Bede's source, refers to a persecution in the reign of the Emperor Septimus Severus. This would give us a date around 209. Some scholars suggest a third persecution: Decius' around 251. Whatever is the date, certainly by the early fifth century, pilgrims were praying at the martyr's tomb and as Bede comments: 'the working of frequent miracles continues to bring it renown.' His shrine survived until the dissolution of St Alban's Abbey in 1539.

Viewers of this picture in Rome would have been taught that England was no less glorious than the Eternal City for the witness of her early martyrs. William Good's interest, however, was the miracles. First we have the river stopping, which Bede says has 'left behind a witness of its ministry.' Then the soldier is healed, having embraced the relic of St Alban's head. Finally, Good points out, that because of St Alban's witness and miracle, the soldier receives baptism in his own blood. Bale had celebrated St Alban and all the traditional pre-St Augustine English martyrs. But he argued in his work on Anne Askew, that they had witnessed to a non-papal church and did not work miracles; they were simply faithful believers in Christ whose purpose in dying had been to allow the community to see 'the strong

workynge of faythe, & beholde the myghte mageste of God in their agonyes.' In emphasizing the miraculous, however, Good is reminding the viewer that miracles are one of the signs of the true Church. St Alban had died in union with the See of Peter for a people still pagan and so miracles, as Bede records, were worked. But did Good omit Bede's reference to the executioner's eyes literally popping out because, like Foxe, he felt that such wonders 'seem more legend-like than truth-like'?

D.   St Julius and St Aaron, with many others, are cut down for the faith.

The martyrdoms of St Julius and St Aaron are very much a background detail to the scene. Bede records that about the time of St Alban's martyrdom, 'Aaron and Julius, both citizens of the city of Legions, suffered, and many others of both sexes in various places. They were racked by many kinds of torture and their limbs were indescribably mangled but, when their sufferings were over, their souls were carried to the joys of the heavenly city.'

Their earthly city may have been Caerleon in Monmouthshire; remains of a Roman amphitheatre, baths and army barracks survive. The martyrs' chopped off limbs, hanging from a tree, would have reminded the seminarians of similar scenes in Elizabethan England.

A | S. Amphibalum, qui S. Albanum baptizarat, du͞ mille homines concionantem audiunt interficiuntur.

B | S. Amphibalus ilia sua palo alligata cultris infixis circumeundo extrahere compellitur, tum Saxis percussus animam Deo, cunctis eam inspectantibus reddidit.

C | Populus tanta martyris constantia ad Christum conversus trucidatur.

PICTURE IV

A.   Two thousand men, on hearing a sermon by St Amphibalus, who had baptized St Alban, are killed.

B.   St Amphibalus is tied to a stake and pierced with knives and has to release himself by the movement of his body. He is then pelted with stones, and surrenders his soul to God in the presence of many watchers.

C.   The people are converted to Christ by the great constancy of the martyrs, and they in their turn are killed.

This picture is a massacre, centred on St Amphibalus, the priest whom St Alban had saved. Thousands are shown dying for the Faith, converted by St Amphibalus' preaching and constancy. The details of his life, however, are a fiction, except that we know St Alban hid a priest, who disappears from the story after his neophyte's arrest. In 1135 Geoffrey of Monmouth gives the priest a name – Amphibalus. It is conjectured that from his reading of an account of Alban's martyrdom by the fifth- or sixth-century writer Gildas, he somehow thought that the word for the priest's cloak – *caracalla* – which St Alban wore to confuse the soldiers, was the priest's name. He then rendered the word in its Latinized Greek equivalent *amphibalus* and it stuck. Further

details appeared after St Amphibalus' relics were 'discovered' on 25 June, 1178, at Redbourn, a few miles from St Albans. A later account recorded how this discovery had been made: St Alban had appeared in a vision to a pious local man, Robert Mercer, indicating where St Amphibalus lay with his martyr companions, and told him that the time had come for them to be venerated. So they were found, exhumed and honoured with a shrine at St Alban's abbey. Perhaps the vision inspired later references to a much earlier appearance of the heavenly Alban to St Amphibalus himself which is shown in our picture. After the discovery, William of St Albans produced a much more embellished life of St Alban and St Amphibalus, which was elaborated even further in the early fifteenth century. The scenes of this picture are found in these works.

William Good does something particularly clever in this scene: he appropriates Protestant criteria for a good minister and true martyrdom. First he stresses that two thousand are converted because of St Amphibalus' preaching. As a young man, George Gilbert had attended

the sermons of the Puritan preacher, Edward Derling, who had taught that preaching was an essential mark of the true church. Good then refers to further conversions, not because of miracles at the martyr's death but, as would please Bale, because of the constancy of St Amphibalus and his companions. Preaching and constancy were no less important to the Church than miracles, and unlike acts of God, could be practised by seminarians.

A | Constantinus in Anglia natus ibique Imperator creatus, visa Cruce, de coelo
audit In hoc Signo Vinces, et Maxentio superato Romam liberat.
B | Idem a Silvestro P.P. baptizatur, et a Lepra sanatur, tum ecclesiā
templis, immunitatibus, et muneribus maximis ornat.

PICTURE V

A.   Constantine is born in England and made Emperor there. He overcomes Maxentius and frees Rome on seeing the Cross, and hearing from heaven 'In this sign you will conquer'.

B.   Constantine is baptized by Pope Sylvester and cured of leprosy. He shows favour to the Church by bestowing on her buildings, privileges and many gifts.

Constantine the Great was not born in England, despite the claim of Geoffrey of Monmouth, but he was proclaimed emperor in the city of York. He was born in 272 or 273 at modern day Niš in Serbia, to Constantius Chlorus and St Helena. For the sake of good government, in 285, the Emperor Diocletian divided in two the vast Roman Empire, making his colleague Maximian co-Emperor in the West. In 293 he created two new posts, two Caesars (junior emperors). Constantius was appointed Caesar with care for the Northwest of the Empire and his son Constantine was sent to Diocletian's court to be educated and, implicitly, as an honoured hostage to ensure his father's loyalty. In 305, Diocletian and Maximian resigned and Constantius, with the Caesar in the East, Galerius, became the new co-Emperors. Fearful of his own safety, Constantine left the Eastern Imperial Court and by the summer had reached his father at modern day Boulogne and crossed with him to Britain. They spent the rest of the campaigning season fighting the Picts. Their time together was short. On 25 July, 306, Constantius died in York. The army in that far-away city, though he was not a Caesar, immediately proclaimed Constantine emperor.

The retired Emperor Maximian's son, Maxentius, was furious with Constantine's claim of the imperial purple; in Rome, in October 306, he declared himself to be the emperor in the West. Constantine, however, remained aloof from direct war with this rival Emperor until 311, when Maxentius declared war on him. After many military successes, Constantine finally faced Maxentius in battle north of Rome at Milvian

Bridge on 28 October 312. In the background of our painting you can see the rival armies engaging battle before the bridge. There are two accounts of Constantine's famous vision before the battle. The oldest is by Lactantius, a Christian apologist and tutor of Constantine's son, Crispin. He records that on the eve of the battle, Constantine had a dream in which he was commanded to put the chi-rho monogram of Christ on the shields of his soldiers. But Eusebius of Caesarea, the first author of a church history, writing in the mid-330s, places the vision earlier, somewhere between 306 and 312 and, according to Eusebius, he learned the details from Constantine himself. Eusebius' vague dating of the vision means that it is possible to speculate that Constantine had it while in England. This is Eusebius' description of the incident:

> This God he began to invoke in prayer, beseeching and imploring him to show him who he was, and to stretch out his right hand to assist him in his plans. As he made these prayers and earnest supplications there appeared to the Emperor a most remarkable divine sign. If someone else had reported it, it would perhaps not be easy to accept; but since the victorious Emperor himself told the story to the present writer a long time ago, when I was privileged with his acquaintance and company, and confirmed it with oaths, who could hesitate to believe the account, especially when the time which followed provided evidence for the truth of what he said? About the time of the midday sun, when day was just turning, he said he saw with his own eyes, up in the sky and resting over the sun, a cross shaped trophy formed from light, and a text attached to it which said, "By this conquer". Amazement at the spectacle seized both him and the whole company of soldiers which was accompanying him on a campaign he was conducting somewhere, and witnessed the miracle.

That evening as Constantine slept, Eusebius tells us, he dreamt of Christ who told him to use the symbol he had seen as protection for his army.

The next morning, Constantine commissioned goldsmiths and jewellers to make a standard with a cross combined with the chi-rho monogram of Christ. Having told his counsellors about his dream, those who were Christian explained: 'the God was the Only-begotten Son of the one and only God, and that the sign which appeared was a token of immortality, and was an abiding trophy of the victory over death.' Eusebius, himself, later saw this bejewelled standard, which had been carried into battle. Constantine was victorious at Milvian Bridge; Maxentius, fleeing, drowned in the Tiber. By 324, three other rivals had been defeated, leaving Constantine as sole Emperor.

Constantine's baptism is an extraordinary moment in world history: the first Roman Emperor to acknowledge Christ and seek salvation from him after three centuries of emperors declaring themselves to be the son of god and Saviour of the World. His baptism, however, did not happen as our painting depicts. Almost immediately after his victory Constantine proves himself to be a great friend and patron of Christianity. As William Good records he bestowed on the Church 'buildings, privileges and many gifts.' Yet he delayed his baptism and, though it would have been fitting that Sylvester, as pope from 314 until only two years before Constantine's own death in 337, should baptize him, it did not happen. Constantine was baptized just before his death at Nicomedia by its bishop, Eusebius. This delay has been viewed by later commentators as a lack of commitment to Christianity or as an almost cynical attempt to control God's forgiveness. Eusebius of Caesarea's account, however, gives this impression: Constantine was so aware of the awesomeness of the gift of baptism that he had a proper fear of the Lord before the sacramental waters.

Eusebius' *Life of Constantine*, written in Greek, was not so well known by the Church in the West as in the East until the late Middle Ages.

At Rome, the alternative history of this period, *Actus beati Silvestri*, written by the early sixth century, became the official story and explains Good's representation. According to the *Actus*, after the year 324, Christians were once more persecuted and Pope Sylvester, with his clergy, fled Rome and hid. Constantine was then struck down by leprosy. No one could heal him but the Capitoline priests bade him visit the Capitol and there bathe in the blood of infants. Distraught, mothers brought their children to be slaughtered. Constantine, appalled by the priests' cruelty and overcome by religious feelings, stopped his carriage on the way to the Capitol and declared this was no way for a valiant soldier to be cured. He had the children returned to their mothers and that night St Peter and St Paul appeared to him in a vision. They told him that Christ, because of his noble action, wished him to send for Sylvester and be healed through baptism. The pope was brought to the palace expecting martyrdom but instead was told of Constantine's vision. Sylvester explained that St Peter and St Paul were not gods but Apostles and enrolled the emperor as a catechumen ordering him to repent and fast. On the Easter Vigil, in the baths of the Lateran Palace, Sylvester baptized Constantine. His leprosy was washed away with his sins.

How the spiritual authority of popes and the temporal authority of kings worked in relation to each other had long been contested. In Foxe's first edition of *Acts and Monuments* (1563), the imagery of the initial letter C praised Elizabeth I as a second Constantine governing a Christian empire – this imperial claim had been adopted by her father – while a toppled pope with shattered tiara and broken keys is depicted lying beneath her throne. The account of Constantine's baptism by Sylvester was a proven response by the Church to such presumptuous monarchs. The emperor may have had a role of great importance in the Church but he knelt to the pope.

A | S. Helena Coeli Regis Angliae filia, Constantini Imperatoris mater
Hierosolymis Christi Crucem effodi iubet.

B | E tribus inventis Crucibus, Machario episcopo suadente, quae
vera Christi sit curationis miraculo dignoscitur.

PICTURE VI

A.   St Helen, daughter of King Coel of England and mother of the Emperor Constantine, goes to Jerusalem, and orders the excavation of the Cross of Christ.

B.   Three crosses are found, but on the advice of Bishop Macharius, the true Cross of Christ is detected by a miraculous cure.

On the top of Colchester Town Hall stands a statue of St Helen. She surveys the oldest recorded town in England. For many years St Helen was celebrated as an Essex woman but she was born nowhere near to its mud flats. She was first given to this island by Henry of Huntingdon, historian and poet, in his truly great history of the English People. He wrote that she was the daughter of Coel, the legendary king of Colchester and of nursery rhyme fame. Geoffrey of Monmouth, somewhat predictably, took this idea and ran with it, writing that the future emperor, Constantius Chlorus, had come to England as a legate of the Roman senate, seized the British kingship on Coel's death, and married Helen, with whom he had Constantine.

In reality, St Helen was probably born into a poor family around the year 248 in modern Herkes in Turkey. While working at an inn, she met the young aristocrat Constantius and became his mistress (she was probably too low socially for him to marry). Their one recorded child is Constantine. St Helen disappears from sight after Constantius marries the daughter of the senior Emperor Maximian but reappears when her son becomes emperor. Sometime after the Battle of Milvian Bridge, Constantine converted his mother to Christianity and established her with great honour in Rome. When he became the sole emperor in 324, Constantine declared her to be the First Woman of the empire. In 326 or 327, St Helen travelled to the Holy Land as a pilgrim and to survey the new churches that Constantine had commissioned for places associated with Christ. She died a year or two later.

Constantine had ordered the Bishop of Jerusalem, St Macarius, to

look for the Cross of Christ. The sites of Golgotha and the Holy Sepulchre were uncovered by removing the Temple of Venus and its terrace which the Emperor Hadrian had had built two hundred years before. St Helen is shown to the left in the painting, standing within the ruins of the temple as workmen excavate for the Cross. We know that around 345, St Cyril of Jerusalem refers to the wood of the Cross, remarking: 'It has been distributed fragment by fragment, from this spot and has already filled the world.' So the Cross was discovered but St Helen's finding it or at least her presence at its discovery is not mentioned until an ecclesiastical history of around 390 by Gelasius of Caesarea. Many, therefore, have written her out of the history. Gelasius, however, was a nephew of St Cyril and potentially well informed about Jerusalem, and St Ambrose links St Helen to the finding of the Cross in a sermon at Milan in 395. Yet it is odd that any record of the Empress' involvement should have remained solely oral for sixty years.

A number of versions of St Helen and the finding of the Cross developed. William Good follows an account by the late fourth-, early fifth-century monk and historian Rufinus, who may have been following Gelasius. He wrote that St Helen had found crosses but could not identify Christ's. Rufinus continues:

> It happened that in the city there was a woman lying ill, nigh unto death. Macarius was bishop of the church at the time. When he saw the empress and the rest standing by, he said, "Bring hither all the crosses that have been found, and God will show us which it was that bore the Lord." Then having entered with the empress and the others into the house of the woman who was ill, he knelt down and prayed thus: "O God, who through thine only-begotten Son

hast inspired the heart of thine handmaid to seek the holy wood upon which our salvation depends, show plainly which cross was identified with the glory of the Lord and which served for the punishment of slaves. Grant that as soon as the health-giving wood touches this woman who is lying half-dead, she may be recalled to life from the gates of death." When he had spoken these words, he touched her with one of the crosses – and nothing happened. Then he applied the second – equally without effect. As soon, however, as he touched her with the third cross, she started up open-eyed and, with her strength fully restored, began to glorify God and to run about the house with greater agility than before her illness. The empress, having obtained her desire through such a clear indication, erected with royal pomp a marvellous temple on the spot where she had found the Cross.

Good's depiction of St Helen emphasises that though she was an empress, she was also, like her son, a good child and servant of the Church. He is, perhaps, also affirming the truth of the relics of the Cross, which were honoured in Rome but had been ridiculed in Reformation England.

S. Vrsula Deonoti Cornubiae in Anglia reguli filia cum undecim
millibus virginum prope Coloniam Agrippinam ab Hunnis pro
Christi fide et virginitate servanda, partim in Rheno mersae, partim
sagittis confixae duplices palmas adeptae sunt.

PICTURE VII

St Ursula, daughter of the ruler Deonotus of Cornwall, and eleven thousand virgins, gain a double martyrdom near Cologne, at the hands of the Huns. For faith in Christ and to preserve their virginity, some were drowned in the Rhine, others shot with arrows.

Cologne sits beautifully upon the Rhine. At the front, in the centre, St Ursula kneels, an arrow through her neck. Behind, a company of thousands wait to be martyred by bow, sword or Rhenish waters. St Ursula was a popular saint on the continent; despite her British origins, less so in England. But then she was a German creation and all we really know about her is that she was probably not called Ursula.

The germ of her story is a memorial stone, seemingly from about the year 400, in a Cologne church, which is now dedicated to her. Its inscription purports to explain that a Christian, Clematius, had restored the church, which was sanctified by the relics of several anonymous virgin martyrs. There is no reference to an Ursula. Her name first appears in a litany datable to 946-962, and soon after a 'history' from Cologne appears with her as the principal heroine. It is in that history that she is given an unnamed British royal father, and the basic details of her life, which through the centuries will be greatly elaborated, are first presented: her dismay at a proposed marriage; her setting off to sea in a flotilla of eleven ships, each holding a thousand virgins; their adventures, including a visit to the tombs of the Apostles in Rome; and their martyrdom at Cologne by the pagan Huns, whose chief St Ursula had refused to marry. The 'history' dates the martyrdoms to 451 'when Attila and his Huns were retreating after their defeat in Gaul; having captured Cologne, then a flourishing Christian city, the first victims of their fury were Ursula and her British followers.' The number of St Ursula's companions probably became fixed at 11,000 through the wrong expansion of an abbreviated text which read 'XI MV' into 'undecim millia virgines' (11,000 virgins) instead of 'undecim martyres virgines' (eleven virgin martyrs).

The Cornish connection is introduced by Geoffrey of Monmouth. In his *History of the Kings of Britain* (1136), he writes that a British prince, settled in Brittany, asked the Duke of Cornwall, Deonotus, who had become King of Britain, to send out women as wives for the settlers. Deonotus generously responded by dispatching his daughter, St Ursula, with 11,000 maidens of noble birth and 60,000 of a lesser sort. Their ships as they neared Brittany, however, were scattered by storms and tragically they landed in alien territory where the women were killed by either Hun or Pict. In 1155 a vast collection of bones was found at Cologne. Their immediate identification with St Ursula's companions only increased the popularity of her story.

Bale was particularly cruel in his treatment of St Ursula. He claimed that her cult was founded upon the belief that a group of nuns had successfully rescued the bodies of the dead from the depths of the sea which, he commented, was highly unlikely. The Catholic Church's valuing of virginity and celibacy were disliked by the reformers. Bale accused Catholics of using St Ursula to promote virginity and to construct a false history of the antiquity of celibacy. These early English Christians went on pilgrimage to Rome, admitted Bale, but as they left

the city they were accompanied by bishops, cardinals and members of the papal household. Having left England to become honest wives they had returned, Bale alleged, as 'bishoppes bonilasses or prestes playeferes.'

In this picture, Good restores the good name of St Ursula, celebrating her virginity, martyrdom, devotion to Rome and in some way, missionary endeavour. Her legend ticks all the boxes. St Ursula was also precious to Good as a Jesuit, because the Society had a particular devotion to her. In 1549, the Jesuits were allowed to have the remains from Cologne of two heads of St Ursula's companions for their church in Messina. Jerome Nadal, the superior of the Messina house, informing St Ignatius about his sermon and invocation of the saints on their arrival in Sicily, said that he was consoled at the devotion of the people towards the relics, 'to the confusion of the heretics.'

A S.Gregorius magnus Anglorum Salutis cupidus, cum ad eos missus
   proficisceretur, Romam revocatur.
B Idem iam Pontifex maximus S.Augustinū Italum cū sociis in Angliā mittit.
C S.Augustinus baptizat S.Edilbertum Angliae provinciae Regem.
D S.Germanus Episcopus Gallus, hostes ethnicos in Anglia fugat Crucis
   signo, Letaniasque et Alleluya cantando.

PICTURE VIII

A.   St Gregory the Great, longing for the salvation of the Angles, is sent to them but after setting out is recalled to Rome.

B.   The same St Gregory, now pope, sends the Italian St Augustine with companions to England.

C.   St Augustine baptizes St Ethelbert, king of the province of England.

This is a key picture. In Bede's *History*, this is the founding moment of the Church in England and Wales. Whatever St Lucius may have achieved (or St Peter according to Greek records) had been washed away by the waves of Angles, Saxons and Jutes to the furthest regions of the West. There British Christians remained in their mountain fastnesses, leaving the pagans ignorant of Christ. With St Augustine's mission this all changes. For eighth-century Bede and sixteenth-century Catholic apologists, the year 597 is the new beginning of divine blessing. For Bale, however, 597 is the start of papal tyranny and corruption in the land for, on the basis of his reading of the Book of Revelation and according to Lutheranism, St Augustine is the servant of the Antichrist. In the face of such prejudice, Good can only restate the historical facts, ensuring that the seminarians know them.

St Gregory, the son of a Roman senator, was born around 540. He entered the employment of the state but in 574 he joined a monastery, which he had founded in Rome. Talented, he was not left in peace, and eventually he became one of Rome's seven deacons, a key administrative post, as well as abbot of his monastery. During this time, says Bede, the following happened according to 'a tradition of our forefathers':

> One day, soon after some merchants had arrived in Rome, a quantity of merchandise was exposed for sale in the market-place. Crowds came to buy and Gregory too amongst them. As well as other merchandise he saw some boys put up for sale, with fair complexions, handsome faces, and lovely hair. On seeing them he asked, so it is said, from what region or land they had been brought. He

was told that they came from the island of Britain, whose inhabitants were like that in appearance. He asked again whether those islanders were Christians or still entangled in the errors of heathenism. He was told that they were heathen. Then with a deep-drawn sign he said, "Alas that the author of darkness should have men of so bright of face in his grip, and that minds devoid of inward grace should bear so graceful an outward form." Again he asked for the name of the race. He was told that they were called *Angli*. "Good," he said, "they have the face of angels and such men should be fellow-heirs of the angels of heaven. And what is the name of the king of the land?" He was told that it was Ælle; and playing on the name, he said, "Alleluia! the praise of God the Creator must be sung in those parts."

St Gregory himself wanted to go to England but he was considered too necessary for work in Rome and shortly afterwards, in 590, he was elected pope. Six years later, however, fulfilling his dream, he sent a party of missionary monks, led by St Augustine. To prepare the way, the pope had already entered into correspondence and released Anglo-Saxon slaves. His sending of St Augustine dominates the picture; England, as Pole had said to Parliament in November 1554, has always been dear to the papacy. Perhaps Good had included the cardinals in the scene to encourage the present ones not to forget England's plight.

St Augustine landed on the isle of Thanet, within the kingdom, as

planned, of Ethelbert. He was King of Kent and the third *bretwalda* of England, exercising some form of lordship over the country south of the Humber. Gregory may have hoped that if Ethelbert was converted, the rest of the English would follow. Bede recalls the king's suspicions of the missionaries but by the end of the year he was probably baptized and many of his people followed. As in the picture of King Lucius, Ethelbert kneels before the pope's representative, indicating his submission to papal authority. The religious habits of St Augustine and his companions also remind the viewer that the missionaries were monks, despite the then contemporary

English disdain of them. This baptism was an extraordinary moment. As one early record of saints' lives states: 'Ethelbert was the first Anglo-Saxon king to receive faith in Jesus. From his stock there has arisen a numerous and holy race, which shines with virtue through the whole world.' The Gregorian mission was the beginning of a well-established Church but it would take time to spread, and only did so with the powerful support of the Irish-initiated mission from Iona.

D   St Germanus, Bishop of Gaul, puts to flight the heathen hordes in England, by the sign of the Cross and the singing of Litanies and Alleluia.

St Germanus was born at Auxerre in central Gaul around 378. He studied law in Rome and became Governor of the Armorican (Breton) border province. In 418 he was named Bishop of Auxerre. Only one Briton – Pelagius – has had a heresy named after him. Pelagianism is the belief that humans can take the initial and fundamental step towards salvation by their own efforts; divine grace is not necessary. In the fifth century, British Christians felt overwhelmed by this heresy and requested help from the bishops of Gaul. In response, they sent two bishops, Lupus of Troyes and Germanus, who at a conference at  Verulamium, advised and encouraged the Britons. The bishops then returned home but some time later Pelagianism revived and so, in 447, Germanus and Lupus returned. During this visit, the Saxons and Picts attacked at Eastertide. The Britons turned to Germanus for help. He organised an army, which included men he had just baptised, and placed them in a valley on the enemies' route. Bede records that 'as the enemy approached, confidently believing that their coming was unexpected, the bishops shouted "Alleluia" three times. A universal shout of "Alleluia" followed and the echoes from the surrounding hills multiplied and increased the sound. The enemy forces were smitten with fear . . . they fled hither and thither casting away their weapons and glad even to escape naked from the danger.'

The 'Alleluia' victory happened 150 years before the Gregorian mission. Perhaps, Good placed it in this picture in tribute to St Gregory, who in the slave market had hoped that English soil and sky would hear the Christian Easter cry, 'Alleluia.'

A S. Edoinus Northumbrorum in Anglia primus Rex Christianus, a Penda
  rege impio in acie occisus miraculis claruit.
B S. Oswaldus ejus gentis rex ab eodem in bello necatus multis
  miraculis Christi martyr est declaratus.
C S. Oswinus ibidem Rex proditus lictoribus occurrit, et peremptus
  miranda edit.

PICTURE IX

A.   St Edwin, first Christian king of the Northumbrians in England, is killed in battle by the wicked King Penda, and shines out by his miracles.

'Arma virumque cano,' the Aeneid begins: 'I sing of arms and a man.' Such words are as perfect for this picture as they were for the story of Aeneas. After a wandering, hunted youth, by force of arms in the year 616, Edwin became King of Northumbria and he steadily increased the size and power of that kingdom. Bede writes, 'It is related that there was so great a peace in Britain, wherever the dominion of King Edwin reached, that, as the proverb still runs, a woman with a newborn child could walk throughout the island from sea to sea and take no harm.'

In 624, Edwin married Ethelburga, a Kentish princess, whose family only agreed to the union if she could remain a Christian and if Edwin would consider conversion. She was accompanied by Paulinus, the first Bishop of York, whom Pope Gregory had sent to England in 601. Edwin was hesitant. He thought long and hard about whether he should turn to this new god. However, on the day he survived an assassination attempt, Ethelburga gave birth to a daughter and he permitted the child to be baptized. 'The first of the Northumbrian race', notes Bede, 'to be baptized, together with eleven members of his household.' Edwin then dropped the worship of idols but still he held out. He turned to his advisers. The chief pagan priest, Coifi, said to the king:

> None of your followers have devoted himself more earnestly than I have to the worship of our gods, but nevertheless there are many who receive greater benefits and greater honour from you than I do and are more successful in their undertakings. If the gods had any power they would have helped me more readily.

But perhaps the most persuasive argument was spoken by one of Edwin's thegns:

This is how the present life of man on earth, king, appears to me in comparison with that time which is unknown to us. You are sitting feasting with your ealdormen and thegns in winter time; the fire is burning on the hearth in the middle of the hall and all inside is warm, while outside the wintry storms of rain and snow are raging; and a sparrow flies swiftly through the hall. It enters in at one door and quickly flies out through the other. For the few moments it is inside, the storm and wintry tempest cannot touch it, but after the briefest moment of calm, it flits from your sight, out of the wintry storm and into it again. So this life of man appears but for a moment; what follows or indeed what went before, we know not at all. If this new doctrine brings us more information, it seems right that we should accept it.

So in 627, after eleven years as king, Edwin, with members of his family, all the nobles and many common people, was baptized at York, where Constantine had begun his journey to Christian rule. Edwin was the first non-Kentish ruler to accept Jesus Christ. Six years later, however, he was dead. The Mercian kingdom had become strong under the rule of the pagan Penda and on 12 October 633, on the border between their kingdoms at Hatfield Chase, Penda and St Edwin fought. St Edwin was killed and his whole army slain or scattered. Bale tried to dismiss St Edwin's death as simply a fact of war but he died for his faith, as subsequent miracles proved. Bishop Paulinus fled with the queen by sea to Kent. St Edwin was buried at the royal monastery of Whitby where a cult began. However, it was only when Pope Gregory XIII allowed him to be depicted in this painting that devotion to the king was formally permitted.

B.   St Oswald, king of his people, is killed by the same man in a war, and is shown to be a martyr of Christ by many miracles.

St Oswald was the son of King Ethelfrith, whose death in battle had enabled Edwin to take the Northumbrian throne. After his father's demise he took refuge in Scotland and Ireland and, at the Columban monastery of Iona, was baptized. In 634, a year after Edwin's death, Oswald took the north of Northumbria at a successful battle near Hadrian's Wall, and, with little opposition, seized the rest of the kingdom and became for eight years overlord of England. St Columba's biographer, Adomnán, reports that before the battle Oswald had had a vision of St Columba encouraging him.

Oswald requested a bishop from Iona to continue the evangelization that had begun under Edwin. The first bishop was too severe, so another one was sought. The new one, St Aidan, was quickly loved. St Oswald gave him the island of Lindisfarne and, since Aidan did not speak English, the king acted as his translator. Bede, in particular, records the king's generosity to the poor. On 5 August 642, at Oswestry in Shropshire, Oswald, as Edwin nine years before him, faced in battle Penda of Mercia. The Mercians were again victorious and, as he died, Oswald prayed for the repose of the souls of his fellow soldiers. His body was ritually dismembered to honour Woden; his head, arms and hands were displayed on stakes. A year later Oswald's brother, Oswiu, who would eventually kill Penda, came with an army and reclaimed his brother's body parts. Over time those parts ended up in different places, including continental Europe, where his reputation grew no less than in England. Oswald's head was eventually buried with the body of St Cuthbert in Durham Cathedral. Bede records many miracles from contact with these relics and Oswald was considered for centuries, down to the iconoclasm of the Reformation, to be a powerful intercessor.

C. St Oswin, king of the same territory, is betrayed and falls into the hands of assassins, and after his death works miracles.

Bede writes that 'King Oswin was tall and handsome, pleasant of speech, courteous in manner, and bountiful to nobles and commons alike.' His father, Osric, the king of Deria, the southern part of Northumberland, was overthrown in 634 and Oswin fled south. In 642, after the death of his brother St Oswald, Oswiu became king of the northern part of

Northumberland, Bernicia, and tried to control the southern kingdom as well. Two years later, however, Oswin successfully claimed Deria, becoming its last independent ruler. He was a great friend to the Church and honoured St Aidan, despite the saint's close ties to Bernicia. At one time, Aidan gave to a poor man a horse, which had been a gift from Oswin. The king was greatly displeased but Aidan corrected him for his lack of care for his fellow man. After some thought, Oswin threw himself at the bishop's feet in sorrow for his words, and promised never again to question his actions. This alarmed Aidan as it probably did Bede; in this world of battles, kings had to show no weakness or submission.

In 651, Oswiu moved against Oswin and, realising that he was greatly outnumbered, Oswin disbanded his army to prevent another Northumbrian bloodshed. Accompanied by a single trusted soldier, he hid in the house of his best friend Hunwald. This thegn, however, betrayed him to Oswiu, who had Oswin and the soldier murdered. His burial place was forgotten during the time of Viking raids but it was rediscovered in 1065 at Tynemouth, a former Bernician monastic site near Newcastle. This led to a renewed devotion to the king and miracles were attributed to him. St Oswin was treated as a martyr because, as a twelfth-century homilist explained, he died 'if not for the faith of Christ, at least for the justice of Christ.' His shrine was destroyed by reformers in 1539.

The events of this picture are a celebration of the royal martyr saints of Northumberland. We shall see more royal martyrs from other Anglo-Saxon kingdoms; no other country has a history of so much royal blood spilt for Christ. Yet in recent decades this period of our history has been ignored and forgotten in schools. Good's celebration of these rulers was a reproof to the Tudor monarchs who had forsaken the Church for which their royal predecessors had died. And, in a litany-like fashion, Good repeats the reputations of these royal saints for miracles. These divine acts are given as evidence that England did not have an earlier hidden non-Roman Church, for miracles are a special blessing for the conversion of pagans. They also demonstrate that the post-Gregorian Church, whether the missionaries came from Kent or Iona, was the true Church.

A SS. duo Sacerdotes Angli Hewaldi nomine, dum Christum Frisonibus
    praedicant, alter gladio confoditur, alter immaniter trucidatur.
B S. Chenelmus rex Midel Anglorum puer septennis i sylva ab educatore
    suo impie occisus, miraculis illustratur.
C Duo fratres Arnaldi Vectae Insulae reguli mox a baptismo decollantur.

PICTURE X

A.   Two holy English priests, Hewald by name, preach Christ to the Frisians, and one is pierced with a sword, the other savagely cut down.

Willibrord was born in Christian Northumbria in 658. Twenty years later, for political reasons, he went to Ireland into exile and studied the Scriptures. Twelve years after that, having been ordained a priest, he returned to England but then decided to become a missionary to the Frisians, a people who lived along the coastland facing England of what is now the Netherlands and Germany. He was joined, among others, by two fellow Northumbrian priests and exiles in Ireland, both called Hewald. To distinguish them, as can be seen in our painting, one was called Hewald the White for his blond hair and the other Hewald the Black for his dark hair. Hewald the Black was particularly learned in the Scriptures. The two Hewalds settled inland in Westphalia, spending their time in prayer and celebrating Mass on their portable altar. Bede tells us that the pagans, fearing that the priests would convert their chief and take away their old religion, killed them; Hewald the White quickly by sword, but Hewald the Black slowly with torture and by tearing his limbs. This happened near Dortmund. Their bodies were thrown into the Rhine. Recovered, they were later enshrined by Pepin III, the father of Charlemagne, in the church of St Cunibert in Cologne, where they still lie. The two Hewalds are the patron saints of Westphalia. For William Good, despite Bale's specific repudiation of them, their missionary work and martyrdoms proved the Anglo-Saxon Church's connection to the universal Catholic Church.

B.   St Kenelm, king of the Middle English, a seven-year-old, is wickedly killed in the forest by his teacher, and is illustrious for miracles.

St Kenelm was the son of King Cenwulf of Mercia, whom he succeeded in

821, when only seven years old. His sister, Cwenthryth, goaded his tutor, Escberht, into killing him. While hunting with Kenelm in a wood, Escberht beheaded him and buried the body at Clent (now in Worcestershire). Cwenthryth became queen. Miraculously, however, a dove delivered a parchment to Pope Leo III in Rome, which told him that Kenelm had been decapitated and was buried under a thorn tree at Clent. The Pope sent legates to the English bishops, ordering them to recover the remains. They did so and carried them to Winchcombe, in the Cotswolds, to be enshrined, for, having died unjustly and as an innocent, Kenelm was judged a martyr. As the relics were carried to the church, his sister stood at a window reciting the psalms backwards as a curse. For this she was punished by both her eyes dropping out onto the page. That is the story of St Kenelm according to a mid-eleventh-century life. As proof of its veracity, his sister's blood-stained psalter was displayed at Winchcombe.

We know that there was a Kenelm, who witnessed a number of charters, almost entirely for King Cenwulf, from 803-811. In Latin he was styled prince or duke. He did not, however, succeed Cenwulf and he had to be older than sixteen to act as a witness. Therefore, Kenelm was probably a member of the royal house of Mercia, who died in the early ninth century and was laid to rest at Mercia's royal burial place at Winchcombe. By the late tenth century, for reasons lost to us, he began to be honoured as a royal martyr-saint. The details of his life, as we have seen, evolved. William of Malmesbury, writing in the early twelfth century, reported that 'the little saint's body is solemnly revered, and hardly anywhere else in England is venerated by a greater throng of people attending a festival.' Chaucer alludes to him in *Canterbury Tales*.

C. Two brothers of Aruald, ruler of the Isle of Wight, are beheaded right after their baptism.

Ceadwalla, king of the Gewisse, from 685, pursued a policy of controlling England south of the Thames. As part of this, he invaded in 686 the Isle of Wight, the last pagan outpost of England. Ceadwalla killed its ruler, Aruald, but two of his brothers escaped to the mainland. They were soon captured but, before they were executed, a local abbot successfully interceded for their eternal salvation: Ceadwalla allowed them to be instructed in the Christian faith and baptized before being killed. In thanksgiving for his capture of  the Isle, the king gave a generous portion of it to the Church. This consideration to the two brothers and the gift of land is remarkable because Ceadwalla was not yet a Christian. He had, however, come under the Church's influence and in 688 he abdicated to travel to Rome to be baptized. He was the first Anglo-Saxon king to come to the Eternal City. On 10 April 689, Pope Sergius I baptized him and gave Ceadwalla the baptismal name Peter. He died ten days later and was buried at St Peter's in his baptismal robes. Bede records the epitaph on his tomb:

His high estate, wealth, kin, a mighty crown,
His strongholds, chieftains, spoils, his high renown
And that of all his sires, Ceadwalla forsook,
Inspired by love of Heaven, that he might look,
A pilgrim king, on Peter and his shrine.

A Sancti tres nepotes S Sigfridi Epi Angli in Suetia occisi sunt, eorum capita
in paludem demersa, illi noctu per lucem Deus ostendit.
B S. Clintaucus rex Suthurallorum in Anglia, ex insidiis peremptus,
miraculis claruit.
C SS. Liuinus epus, Liuina virgo, Socrates et Stephanus Angli, diuersis
temporibus, mortem pro Christo subeunt.

PICTURE XI

A. The three holy nephews of St Sigfrid, an English bishop, are killed in Sweden. Their heads are sunk in the marsh, but God shows him by a light where to find them.

St Sigfrid has one of the more unusual iconographies: three heads in a box. They belonged to his nephews, who were martyred supporting his missionary endeavours. The earliest life we have of Sigfrid comes from the late twelfth century. He may have been a monk of Glastonbury, whom King Ethelred the Unready chose to be ordained as a bishop and

sent as a missionary to King Olav Tryggvason of Norway. Sigfrid moved on, however, to Sweden and, some time at the beginning of the eleventh century, baptized its ruler, Olav Skötkonung.

According to tradition, St Sigfrid had taken with him three nephews, Unaman, Sunaman and Vinaman, who mhe left in charge of his newly-established diocese while he set out to evangelize more distant provinces. While Sigfrid was away, they were murdered by a gang, who cut off their heads, threw them into a pond in a box, and buried their bodies in the forest. As William Good tells us, their heads were revealed by a divine light, which in the picture is shown as a flame. Such a divine light revealed the location of St Kenelm's head. The recovered heads were placed in a shrine. Sigfrid protected the murderers from the fullness of the king's justice, having their death sentences commuted to heavy fines. He died around 1045 after many years of missionary work in both Sweden and Denmark. Until the Reformation, Sigfrid was held in high regard in Sweden – he was considered their apostle. This is another example of the international missionary endeavour of the Anglo-Saxon Church, which, strikingly this time, was initiated by the king himself. The divine illumination of the nephews' heads not only reveals their murders but enables their heads to be venerated as relics and so, therefore, we could conclude, this is a divinely blessed practice.

B.   St Clitaucus, king of the Suthuralli in England, is treacherously killed, and is famous for his miracles.

St Clitaucus or Clydog, like St Oswin and St Kenelm, is a betrayed royal martyr; a feature of Anglo-Saxon saints' lives. The little we know of him comes from the Book of Llan Dav, which was written around 1150, six hundred years or so after St Clitaucus is meant to have lived. According to this account, St Clitaucus was of the Brychan family and ruled modern-day Herefordshire and Monmouthshire. He fell in love with a nobleman's daughter and determined to marry her. But one of his comrades was a rival suitor and, while out hunting, the man killed his king by the sword. The body was then placed on a cart and driven to a ford in the river Monnow. However, the yoke broke and the oxen refused to go further, so a church was built there for the burial of St Clitaucus. Richard Whytford, the learned Bridgettine monk, who was a friend of Erasmus and More, described the saint as 'a kynges son of strayte iustyce, a louer of peace, and of pure chastite, and of strayte and perfyte life yᵗ was cruelly slayne by a fals traytour at whose deth were shewed many myracles and at his tombe after many moo.'

C.   St Livinus, bishop, St Livina, virgin, Saints Socrates and Stephen, all English, are put to death for Christ at different times.

The eleventh century life of St Livinus states that his father was a Scots noble and his mother came from a royal Irish family; not English, therefore, as Good states. He was baptized by St Augustine of Canterbury,

who later ordained him. Later still he became a bishop and, with three companions, he preached to the pagans of Brabant, who cut off his head at Eschen, near Alost. It has been proposed, however, that St Livinus may not have existed but tales of him arose from confusion with the story of a real English missionary: St Liafwine or Lebuin. This saint was a monk from Ripon Monastery who, in 754, went as a missionary to Frisia – like the two St Hewalds – and Germany. St Liafwine, however, was neither ordained a bishop, nor martyred. Somehow, in whatever sources Good was using, the real saint and probably imaginary one had been confused.

There is no record of the history of St Socrates and St Stephen. Some have conjectured that they suffered at the same time as St Alban and, perhaps, in Monmouthshire or South Wales, where churches are dedicated to them. Martyrologies, which have recorded the place of their martyrdoms as in *Britannia* (in Britain), however, may have erred. Perhaps they should have stated in *Bithynia*, an ancient Roman Province of Asia Minor.

Perhaps appropriately for this disappointing picture of saints, I have been unable to find any references to the virgin and martyr, St Livina. Bale's attacks upon such saints as St Ursula or St Thomas of Canterbury were suggestive and crude. He would not have been wrong, however, to question the existence of some of them.

A | S. Georgius Cappadox Dracone occiso, Regis filiam, totamque Silenam
civitatem mortis periculo liberat, et ad Christum convertit.
B | Idem Veneno hausto, corpore lacero, ignitis calceis indutus, plumboque
perfusus, capite praeciso invictus Christi miles coronatur.
| Hunc clarissimum martyrem Anglia sibi protectorem elegit, et
maximis beneficiis tum pace tum bello receptis, semper religiosissi
me coluit.

PICTURE XII

A. St George from Cappadocia, having killed the dragon, frees the king's daughter and the whole city of Silene from danger of death, and converts them to Christ.

B. The same St George, having been given poison, his body mangled, placed on burning coals and covered in lead, and his head cut off, is crowned as an unconquered soldier of Christ. England has adopted this most splendid martyr as her Protector, has always had great devotion to him, and has received great blessings as a result both in war and peace.

St George was a Palestinian martyr of the early fourth century, who may have been a soldier. He suffered at Lydda, which claimed to have his tomb. Devotion to him was ancient and widespread; he was sought often as an intercessor. The suggestion that St George was Cappadocian is probably an early confusion between him and another George who was from Cappadocia but was an Arian heretic who opposed St Athanasius.

Nature abhors a vacuum and to the little that was known of him, much through the centuries was added. George's rescue of a princess from a dragon does not appear before the tenth century but when it was included in the account of his life in the mid-thirteenth-century book of saints' lives, the *Golden Legend* – an enormously popular work – it became his principal adventure. The basic details are that a water-dwelling dragon had been threatening a town, usually called Silene, in Libya. To keep it away the citizens fed it with sheep. When they began to run out of this woolly quadruped, they agreed among themselves to sacrifice one child and one sheep each day. Lots were drawn, and eventually the king's only daughter was chosen. The king asked for her to be spared but the people threatened to burn him and his palace if he refused to give her up. So she was led out with her sheep. St George, however, passing by, rescued her by wounding the dragon, and had the princess lead the fiery beast, by a girdle around its neck, back to Silene. There, before the citizens, St George offered to kill the dragon, if they would convert to Christianity. The people accepted and followed their king through the waters of baptism. It is easy enough, of course, to understand the combat with the dragon as a stylised way of representing St George overcoming evil, as every saint must.

Early on in the East, St George was called 'megalomartyros' – martyr among martyrs. Before the dragon appeared, this was the principal reason for celebrating St George: he had died for Christ. Over time, in legends and paintings, the way he died developed, with imaginative torture after torture being added. His eventual and inevitable death by beheading was only one final act after many acts of suffering. Good lists some of the supposed tortures; many others were available. And the dragon, though he became a distraction, never obliterated the emphasis upon, nay seeming delight in, George's sufferings. At the beginning of the sixteenth century, just before the Reformation, the Parish of St Neot in Cornwall had a large window erected in honour of the Christian knight. The dragon gets its moment but six other scenes are dedicated to the torturing of George. He had become, *par excellence*, the model of *imitatio Christi* – of imitating Christ, especially in his patient suffering. What St George was imagined to have gone through was outlandish but, perhaps, for the seminarians inspiring, because their mission to England, and what could happen, was no less outlandish.

St George had been known in England since at least the seventh century but it was through the Crusades that local devotion increased. William of Malmesbury wrote that during the First Crusade, St George and St Demetrius, the martyr knights, had been seen assisting the Crusaders at the Siege of Antioch. At the Third Crusade, Richard I placed himself and his army under George's protection. By now he was established as a patron saint for soldiers and, in 1222, the Synod of Oxford made his day a lesser feast in England. Edward III, in the 1340s, founded, under the patronage of St George, the Order of the Garter. And, finally, in 1415, his feast was made one of the principal celebrations of the English Church following Henry V's invocation of him at the Battle of Agincourt. Good emphasises, in the inscription accompanying this picture, the blessings that England has received from St George. He would surely have been horrified at what had been done in England to his memory.

Some Protestants attributed George's legend and veneration to the Antichrist. William Cecil, Elizbeth I's secretary of state, eradicated all references to St George in the Order of the Garter's revised statutes and removed the dragon from the Garter pendant leaving simply an image of an armed knight on horseback with a drawn sword. In a way, one could be sympathetic with this desire to remove fairytales from Christian devotion but it was more than that. The reformers were eradicating England's heavenly helpers and her past.

This picture – excluding the very final picture – includes the only contemporary likeness, at least that we are aware of, in the wall paintings. In October 1583, the rector of the English College, Alphonso Agazzari, recalled that 'some (students) requested the artist to make the face of St George a portrait of that of George Gilbert, this he already merited, being so like the saint in many respects.' Modestly, Gilbert demurred. Agazzari reports, however, that:

> The artist managed to give to the saint a certain air of resemblance on noticing which he said to the painter, "How is it you have represented a man armed and in the act of fighting without his visor? Pray make this correct." The painter offered some opposition, but it was arranged that he should give the saint a helmet. However, Mr Gilbert was not fully satisfied, and, in order that the face might still more be concealed, he required the two armour side-plates, which usually cover the ears and are tied under the chin, to be added. Father Minister objected and would by no means allow his wishes to be complied with, for he much desired that the portrait of the gentleman should remain in the college for the consolation of all.

A S. Wulstanus duorum regum nepos occiditur, super cuius corpus per

30 dies Lux e coelo micuit.

B Tres simul comites eius passi sunt.

PICTURE XIII

A.   St Wulstan, grandson of two kings, is killed, and for thirty days a light shines on his body from heaven.

B.   At the same time suffer three of his companions.

In Bede's *History*, the King of Mercia, Penda, is the villain. In Picture IX, a celebration of Northumbrian royal martyrs, we saw him dispatch both King Edwin and King Oswald to heaven. The pagan Penda was himself killed in 655 by Oswiu, St Oswald's brother. However, two years before this, Penda's son, Paeda, had chosen to be baptised. This led to the eventual conversion of Mercia. St Wulstan, or more commonly, St Wigstan or St Wistan, was a member of the kingdom's royal house.

The earliest record of St Wigstan's martyrdom is his tomb. In the ninth century, the crypt of the church of Repton, in Derbyshire, was greatly altered to allow the creation of a shrine for his body. In the following years, people vied to have their tombs close to his. The eleventh- and twelfth-century accounts of his life seem to include plenty of authentic ninth-century information and so, with some confidence, we can say (and hopefully without getting too confused by Anglo-Saxon names) that St Wigstan was the son of Wigmund, son of Wiglaf, king of Mercia. On his father's death, for personal religious reasons, St Wigstan refused to become king. A kinsman,

Beorhtfrith, approached St Wigstan's widowed mother, Elfleda, requesting her hand in marriage. St Wigstan persuaded his mother to decline; perhaps because he regarded such a union as incestuous. Beorhtfrith, with malice in his heart, asked to see him. On the saint's arrival, Beorhtfrith rose and, under feint of offering him the kiss of peace, sacrilegiously killed him and three companions. The year was 849. As with the nephews of St Sigfrid in Picture XI, William Good notes that a light from heaven revealed the location of St Wigstan's body. Bede tells us that the same miracle also illuminated the bodies of the two St Hewalds and St Oswald.

St Wigstan's burial place in Repton became a popular place of pilgrimage but, in 1019, the Abbot of Evesham persuaded King Cnut to give him St Wigstan's relics for his monastery. There, in Worcestershire, they became the centre of new devotions and veneration. After the

Conquest, some doubted the miracles claimed for the shrine – a usual Norman dismissal of the Anglo-Saxon saints – and so the new Norman abbot subjected the relics to an ordeal by fire, especially St Wigstan's head. They miraculously emerged unscathed.

A S.Eobanus Traiecti Episcopus martirio coronatur

B S.Adelarius Erfordi Episcopus pro fide occiditur.

   ambo S.^ti Bonifacij episcopi et martiris socij fuere.

PICTURE XIV

A.   St Eoban, bishop of Utrecht, is crowned with martyrdom.

B.   St Adelarius, bishop of Erfurt, is killed for the faith. Both are companions of St Boniface, bishop and martyr.

The names of those who were killed with the Englishman St Boniface (see next picture) at Dokkum in 754 change between the different accounts of the martyrdom. These two have been included in some of the accounts: St Eoban, the Bishop of Utrecht, and St Adelard, the first Bishop of Erfurt. Beyond their sharing the martyr's crown with St Boniface, nothing further is known of them.

A S. Bonifacius Anglus Moguntiae Archiepiscopus in Frisia Christum
 docens simul cum tribus monachis Anglis interimitur.
B S. Ositha Virgo, et martyr caput abscissum per mille passus gestat.
C S. Æthelbertus estanglorum rex, insidiis Vxoris regis Offae e cubiculo
 superiore perforato, et operto lecto decidit, et a nefariis hominibus
 trucidatus Christi martyr efficitur.

PICTURE XV

A. St Boniface, an Englishman, Archbishop of Mainz, teaches about Christ in Friesland and is killed with three English monks.

St Boniface is, perhaps, the greatest English saint to have worked on the continent – he reformed and organised the Church across much of north-western Europe – and he won a martyr's crown. In 1603, Robert Persons described him as 'the most famous Saint and Martyr of all the rest of our nation.' Bale, however, vilified him as 'one of the two hornes of the beast described in the Apocalips'.

Boniface was born around 672-675 near Exeter. His parents named him Wynfreth. Placed as a child-oblate in a monastery near his birth-place, he later moved to the monastery at Nursling, close to Southampton, where at thirty years old he was ordained and became the head of the monastic school. His ambition, however, was to be a missionary and, in 716, he went to Frisia, to continue the earlier work of the English missionary Willibrord, who had been accompanied by the two martyred Hewalds. Yet the political situation was not good: the king of the Frisians, Radbod, had turned against Christians and Wynfreth soon realised that he would not be able to achieve much. So he returned home, was elected Abbot of Nursling, declined the honour and, in 718, set off for Rome.

Other Anglo-Saxon missionaries had been to Rome before but, to Bale's chagrin eight hundred years later, Wynfreth would build up especially close links with the papacy and, through his missions, would improve the Holy See's own links with emerging and developing Christian communities. The pope, Gregory II, received Wynfreth warmly, gave him a new name – Boniface – and commissioned him to preach in Bavaria and, to the north-west, in Hesse. Meanwhile, however, conditions had improved in Frisia – Radbod had died. So Boniface pursued his original plan and returned for three years to the Frisians.

Finally arriving in Hesse, Boniface learnt of the oak tree of Geismar, sacred to Thor, a sign of the power of the old gods. He took an axe and felled the oak; faith in the gods came crashing down with it. Now a bishop, in Hesse, and also to the west in Thuringia, Boniface refuted paganism, encouraged those who were wavering in their Christianity and founded monasteries, staffed with English monks and nuns, as missionary centres. Then in 738, Charles Martel, ruler of the Franks, a Christian and the grandfather of Charlemagne, defeated the Saxons of Westphalia. This left these cousins of the English, in their defeat, open to missionaries. Boniface wrote to the people of England asking for their prayers and help in the conversion of those who 'are of one blood and bone with you.' But Charles Martel failed to hold on to his successes and Westphalia was lost. So instead of working there, Boniface returned to Bavaria and reorganised its dioceses. During the 740s he built up the Church of the Frankish Kingdom, which was increasingly gobbling up north-west Europe and, in 746, he became Archbishop of Mainz.

Boniface's life, as these brief and cursory facts tell, was a whirlwind of activity dedicated to the Lord. Yet even in the 750s, now nearly eighty, he did not stop. He travelled once more northwards to the Frisians, to spend his last days with them. He reclaimed the part of the country earlier evangelised and also, with some success, went to pagan north-east Frisia. And then martyrdom came suddenly: when Boniface was awaiting, on the banks of the river Borne near Dokkum, some neophytes for confirmation, a band of pagans attacked and killed him and his companions. As the picture shows, he held up the Book of Gospels, to defend himself from the blows of swords and daggers. His body was taken back to one of his great monastic foundations, Fulda in Hesse.

The Bishops' Conference of Germany has its annual meeting there, to be near the shrine of the Apostle of Frisia and Germany.

Boniface's life, one of the best documented of the eighth century, demonstrates just how integrated the Church in England was with the Church on the continent. English missionaries led the way. From their island they brought what they were – Christians loyal to Peter.

B. St Osyth, Virgin and martyr, is beheaded and carries her head for a thousand paces.

Our knowledge of the seventh-century St Osyth, who is associated with both Essex and Buckinghamshire, is dependent upon two twelfth-century lives, which are themselves only known from later and fragmentary versions. But her story has enough aspects to it which accord with our knowledge of seventh-century south-east England that we can presume that at the heart of the legend there is a real St Osyth.

The most commonly told version of her life depicts her as an Anglo-Saxon princess of the tribe of the Hwiccas. She was married to Sighere, King of the East Saxons (*c.* 664-83), at the direction of his overlord Wulfhere, King of Mercia. Bede records that Sighere apostatised and it is possible that the marriage was arranged to consolidate Christianity among the East Saxons (the people of Essex). We know that Sighere was later reconverted. Bede never makes any mention of St Osyth. Having had one child together, her husband allowed her to found a convent at Chich (later re-named in her honour) on the east coast of Essex where she died around 700 and was later venerated as a saint. There are a number of miraculous events associated with her. Naturally, William Good has included the one associated with the legend of Osyth's martyrdom at Chich at the hands of pirates. They beheaded her when she refused to worship their false gods and, with her head in her hands, St Osyth walked three miles to a church (shown behind her in the picture) where she placed her head on the altar.

Some of the early Norman bishops of London had a particular devotion to her. Maurice (1085-1107) translated her body to a new shrine behind the high altar of the church at Chich. His successor, Richard de Belmeis (1108-1127) founded a priory at Chich of Augustinian Canons to maintain the shrine and to give thanks after recovering from a stroke, which he thought had been caused by St Osyth; a punishment for his alienation of some of her lands for a pleasure park. Bishop Richard later died at Chich and was buried there. It is striking that Norman churchmen, who normally were disdainful of the Anglo-Saxon saints of this conquered isle, should have paid St Osyth so much attention. She was invoked against fire, and the cathedrals of both London and Canterbury claimed to have arm relics.

C.   St Ethelbert, king of the East Angles, when his upper chamber is invaded by the wiles of the wife of King Offa, falls from his bed and is murdered by wicked men, and is thus made a martyr of Christ.

The only pre-conquest reference to St Ethelbert is in the Anglo-Saxon Chronicle for the year 794: 'Offa, king of the Mercians, had Ethelbert beheaded.' We have, however, three lives of St Ethelbert from the twelfth century and one from the thirteenth. From these we can compile an acceptable expansion of the Chronicle's brief statement.

St Ethelbert had become king either because he was of the royal house of the East Angles or because he was of the royal house of Mercia, whose king, Offa, defeated the East Angles. If he was of royal

Mercian blood, Offa, his overlord may have had St Ethelbert killed so that there would be no rival to his own son inheriting the Kingdom of Mercia; or St Ethelbert's minting of coins, a privilege which Offa did not allow normally to his sub-kings, may have made him seem a threat. Either way, a contemporary scholar, Alcuin, observed that Offa pursued a ruthless policy of eliminating rivals and all of the accounts agree that St Ethelbert was beheaded, the traditional punishment for usurpers or would-be usurpers.

The accounts also agree that St Ethelbert was killed at the Mercian royal court near Hereford, having been invited by Offa, who used his daughter's hand in marriage as bait. The thirteenth-century life of St Ethelbert, written at St Albans Abbey, which William Good followed, blames Offa's wife, Cwenthryth, for instigating the murder. The abbey had been founded by Offa; perhaps the monks were keen to clear their founder's name. Yet we know that Cwenthryth was a powerful figure and Offa often sought her advice. The various accounts disagree on the arrangements for the beheading but Good, following again the St Alban's account, has St Ethelbert fall into a pit after sitting on a booby-trapped chair or bed. St Ethelbert, smothered by the drapes of the collapsed bed, is killed. His end is the most Jacobean of all the depicted martyrs.

St Ethelbert's body was buried by the river Lugg at Marden but, as with St Wulstan and St Kenelm, a divine light revealed its burial place and it was translated to Hereford, seven miles away. By the mid-eleventh century, Hereford Cathedral was dedicated to St Ethelbert and his shrine became second only to Canterbury as a place of pilgrimage. As with other murdered royal Anglo-Saxons, you could wonder why St Ethelbert is called a martyr. His cult may have begun as a focus for resistance to Offa's oppressive rule yet the great St Dunstan in the tenth century encouraged devotion to St Ethelbert and many miracles were associated with his shrine.

A S. Ebba Angla regii sanguinis Colinganiensis monasterii abbatissa ne in
   Danorum infidelium libidinem incurrat, nasum et superius labrū
   sibi cultro praescindit eius exemplum reliquae Moniales pro casta
   religione tuenda fortiter sequuntur.
B Omnes Monasterio inclusas ignis ab hoste iniectus tanquam immaculatas
   hostias absumit.
C S. Eugulus Episcopus impie occiditur.
D S. Licfardus Epūs Roma peregrinus rediens Cameraci martyr efficitur.

PICTURE XVI

A.   St Ebba, of royal blood, abbess of the monastery of Coldingham, to escape the lust of the infidel Danes, cuts off her own nose and upper lip with a knife. The other nuns, in order to protect their religious chastity, bravely do the same.

B.   All the inhabitants of the monastery, which is set on fire by the enemy, perish as immaculate sacrifices.

The original St Ebba was the sister of St Oswald, whose martyrdom was depicted in Picture IX. She was the first abbess of a monastery at Coldingham, in Berwickshire, now in Scotland; nearby St Abbs Head is named after her. In 686, a few years after her death, the monastery was destroyed by fire.

According to Matthew Paris, the thirteenth-century chronicler and

monk of St Albans, Coldingham Monastery was later re-founded and, in 870, was attacked by the Danes. The abbess at the time was another St Ebba, styled 'the Younger', to distinguish her from the first. Fearful that the nuns would be raped, she devised an extreme plan to repel the marauders: the community cut open their noses and lips with razors. Circignani depicts the nuns' noses lying on the ground. Indeed, the Danes were so disgusted by the spectacle that they did not harm the community that time but they

soon returned and burnt down the monastery with St Ebba and her companions inside.

Paris may have used an older, lost source from Tynemouth but before his chronicle we have no evidence of this St Ebba; there was no ancient cult. By the thirteenth century, however, there was a shrine. The reference to St Ebba the Younger's royal blood may have arisen from confusing her with St Ebba the Elder.

C.   St Augulus, bishop, is wickedly slain.

According to Stanton's *Menology*, the S. Eugulus of this picture is St Augulus, Bishop of London; there is no other saint of such a similar name who was also a martyred English bishop. It is conjectured, however, that St Augulus died during Emperor Diocletian's persecution. This would mean that William Good has seriously misplaced St Augulus within British history.

D. St Liephard, bishop, goes on pilgrimage to Rome and on his return is martyred at Cambrai.

According to the records of the Diocese of Cambrai, St Liephard was a British bishop, perhaps Welsh, who on his return from Rome, in 640, was martyred by pagan robbers in a wood near Cambrai. His relics were eventually honoured at St Quentin in northern France but were lost at the end of the Spanish siege of that city in 1557.

A S. Edmundus Estangsorum rex ultimus a Danis telis configitur.
B Eidem caput praeciditur, quod procul abiectum dum a sois
   quaeritur ter respondit Hic.
C Eius corpus cum deinde transferretur capiti innctum
   reperitur rubra cicatrice uulnus indicante.
D S. Humbertus Episcopus Halmensis iuxta regem obtruncatur.

PICTURE XVII

A.   St Edmund, last king of the East Angles, is pierced by the Danes with javelins.

B.   St Edmund's head is cut off and thrown far away, but when his friends look for it, it calls 'Here!' three times.

C.   When his body is being moved, it is discovered that it is reconnected to the head, showing the wound of beheading by a red scar.

The Anglo-Saxon Chronicle for 870 records that: 'In this year the raiding (Danish) army took up winter quarters at Thetford. And that winter King Edmund fought against them, and the Danes had the victory, and killed the king and conquered all the land.' Since the Chronicle seems to begin the year on 24 September, Edmund died in 869. He had been brought up as a Christian and he may have become King of the East Angles in 865. This is the little we know about his life but much was written about his death and subsequent events.

The earliest evidence for a devotion to St Edmund is a memorial coinage inscribed 'Scē Eadmund Rex', which was widely current in the Danish-controlled parts of England (the Danelaw) within a generation of his death. Most of the details which are depicted in this picture come from the *Passio sancti Eadmundi*, which was written by St Abbo of Fleury when he was in charge of studies at the monastery school of Ramsey from 985 to 987. He records that he learnt the story of St Edmund's death from St Dunstan, who, in turn, had learnt it from an old man who was St Edmund's armour-bearer on the day the king died.

According to St Abbo, St Edmund did not die in battle. When his lands were threatened by a group of Danes, the king allowed himself to be seized by them in his own Hall rather than engage them in battle and have any of his people killed. The Danes tortured St Edmund to make him forsake Christ. St Abbo explicitly compares the king's last hours and death with those of Christ and St Sebastian: St Edmund was mocked and scourged like Christ, and tied to a tree and shot with arrows like St Sebastian, until he bristled 'like a prickly hedgehog or a spiny thistle.' Yet, St Edmund refused to deny his Saviour so he was unbound and beheaded. This probably happened at Hellesdon, on the outskirts of Norwich.

St Abbo describes what happened next:

> The pirate force went after to the ships and hid the head of Saint Edmund in thick bushes so that it could not be buried. Then, sometime after they were gone, the people of the place, those who were left, came to where their master's body lay without a head and were very sad in heart about his death and especially that they did not have the head for the body. Then the witness [St Edmund's armour-bearer] related what he had seen – that the pirates had taken the head with them; and he thought, as turned out to be true, that they had hidden it somewhere in the forest. They went, all together, to the woods and searched everywhere through bushes and brambles that they might find that head. There was a miracle – a wolf [as shown in the picture] was sent by God's guidance to defend that head, with other wild animals, day and night. They went searching and often calling, as is the custom, through the woods: "Where is our companion now?" And then the head answered "Here, here, here," and as often as they called, it always answered, as often as any of them called out until they all came together through calling to him. There lay a grey wolf that had the head they had looked for, and with his feet he clasped the head, greedy and hungry, and because of God he dared not eat the head but protected it with the wild beasts. Then they were amazed by the wolf's guardianship and journeyed home with the holy head, thanking the Almighty for his wonders.

St Abbo records another miracle from around 915 when the remains of St Edmund's body were examined: 'he was whole, as if he were alive, with unblemished body and his neck uninjured that formerly was cut through – and it was like a silken thread was about his neck, a sign to men of how he was killed.' Good places this miracle immediately after the martyrdom, at the time of the discovery of the head. The miraculous preservation of St Edmund's body led to its translation to Bedricsworth (later called Bury St Edmunds). In 925 a small community of two priests and four deacons was established to take care of the shrine. King Cnut, making reparation for his compatriots' crimes, replaced it in 1020 with Benedictine monks and built a stone church. By the time of the Reformation, Bury St Edmunds had grown to be one of the great shrines and abbeys of England.

Good included St Edmund for three reasons: he was one of the most celebrated martyrs of England, Bale had tried to dismiss him, and he was the patron saint of a Roman hospice for English pilgrims that came to be owned by the English College. In 1396, John Whyte, a London merchant, took over the lease *in perpetuo* of the Hospice of San Crisogono, which stood in front of the Church of San Crisogono in Trastevere, near the River Tiber. The hospice offered accommodation for poor Christians. By 1406 the members of the Confraternity that ran it were all English or Welsh, bar two, and the hospice had become known as 'the English hospital'; by 1445 St Edmund's name had been added to San Crisogono's as a patron. Then, in 1464, the English and Welsh takeover was completed by the union of St Edmund's with the Hospice of St Thomas of Canterbury in via di Monserrato. When that hospice became the English College, St Edmund's became one of the seminary's properties. It was appropriate then that the 1581 altarpiece for the college church should depict, below the Most Holy Trinity, the two patron saints of the English hospices: St Thomas of Canterbury and St Edmund Martyr. Good's almost complete devotion of one picture to St Edmund is an act of piety.

D.   St Humbert, bishop of Elmham, is killed beside the king.

We know little of St Humbert, except that he may have been martyred on the same day as St Edmund. According to St Abbo's description of the king's last day, there was a bishop at hand whose advice he had sought. Elmham was the see for Norfolk, within the Kingdom of the East Angles, from 672 to 1071.

A | S. Sophias ter Hierosolymam, septies Romani religiose peregrinatus. Beneuenti, ubi epūs erat, dum missam celebrat lancea confoditur.

B | S. Fremundus regis filius post uitam in eremo factam capite truncatur.

C | S. Iustinianus monachus caput sibi amputatum tulit, miraculis Meneuiae claruit.

D | S. Melorus septennis a fratre manu et pede altero praeciso adolescens capite plexus martyrium subiit.

Picture XVIII

A.   St Sophias goes on pilgrimage to Jerusalem three times and to Rome seven times. At Benevento, where he is bishop, he is run through with a lance while celebrating Mass.

St Sophias is one of the names given to St Cadoc, the great sixth-century Welsh saint, who was probably a contemporary of St David. It is difficult for us to trust with certainty the details of his life because what we know comes from a late eleventh- or early twelfth-century *Life* by Lifris, though he was probably working from earlier texts, which are now lost.

We are told that St Cadoc was the son of St Gundleus, King of southern Wales, and St Gwladys. He is credited with founding, early in his life, the monastery at Llancarfan, in the vale of Glamorgan; its fame as a place of holiness and learning was immense. The manuscript of Lifris' *Life* also contains an account of the martyrdom of St Cadoc, in which he is transported in a white cloud to Benevento, southern Italy, ordained a bishop and later killed. There are three possible explanations for this version of the end of his life: it may have been devised to explain why Llancarfan did not have his body and to depict him as a bishop; or the Welsh had hidden St Cadoc's relics and the Benevento story was the Anglo-Normans' explanation of their absence; or St Cadoc may have become the bishop at Bennavena (later confused with Benevento) or Weedon, in Northamptonshire, where he was martyred by pagan Anglo-Saxons.

Lifris' *Life* also includes a story of St Gildas going to Rome, where he presented a bell to the pope, explaining that it was last rung in the guest house of St Cadoc. To which the pope replied: 'Some time ago I got to know the man you mention, for he came here as a pilgrim seven times, and three times to Jerusalem, to seek forgiveness for the souls of his parents and kinsmen.'

B. St Fremund, the king's son, spends his life in the wilderness, and is beheaded.

St Fremund's story is obscure. The son of a powerful member of the royal house of Mercia, he became a hermit but left his retreat to defend his religion and his country from the threat of the Danes. He was killed, however, with the help of the Danes, by an apostate kinsman, Oswy, who feared him as a rival to the Mercian throne. He was buried at Offchurch in Worcestershire. In 1212 his relics were translated to Dunstable; the accompanying miracles confirmed his sanctity and increased the popularity of his shrine.

William Good is not just restoring the good name of the saints that the Reformation had tried to eradicate, but also the memory of their shattered shrines.

C. St Justinian, a monk, picks up his own head after it has been cut off. He graces Menevia with miracles.

The cult of St Justinian is ancient. He probably lived during the sixth century. The details of his surviving *Life*, however, can only be traced as far back as the twelfth century. According to this source, St Justinian was a Breton of noble birth and good education. He was ordained a priest and, leaving his country to follow Christ more perfectly, he eventually settled on Ramsey Island, half a mile from St David's Peninsula, the most westerly point of Wales. Honorius, a devout man, already lived there with his sister and her maid. He invited St Justinian to remain but the Breton would only agree to this if Honorius sent away the women. He did so and the two men lived in amity.

St David, learning of St Justinian, had him visit and was so impressed by him that he gave St Justinian houses on the island and the mainland. Later some sailors told St Justinian that St David was ill and offered to take him to the ailing man but as they crossed the waters, the saint realised from their ugliness that the sailors were demons. So he prayed Psalm 79 – 'O shepherd of Israel, hear us' – and the devils 'flew away like black crows.' Having arrived safely, St Justinian found St David in good health.

The demons, however, did not give up. They possessed St Justinian's servants, who were driven into a rage, when the saint told them to work hard. They threw him to the ground and cut off his head; a curative spring of water appeared where it landed. St Justinian's body, like St Osyth's, then carried its head to the place where it wished to be buried. A church was built on the spot. After many miracles there, St David translated the body to a new tomb in his own monastery, around which the town of St David's later developed.

By the Middle Ages, the relics of both saints were venerated in the same shrine and Kings William I, Henry II, and Edward I made pilgrimages there. John Pecham, the thirteenth-century Archbishop of Canterbury, noted an inscription on the saints' shrine which claimed that two pilgrimages to St David's were the equivalent of one to Rome.

The location of St David's monastery, two and a half miles inland from St David's Head, was given by the first monks the Latin name Menevia. This may have reflected its early Welsh name, Mynyw, meaning 'a grove'.

D. St Melorus, at the age of seven, has one hand and one foot cut off by his brother, and as an adolescent undergoes martyrdom by beheading.

William of Malmesbury visited St Melorus' shrine in Amesbury, Wiltshire, in the early twelfth century but he could learn nothing certain as to the saint's race or sanctity. The cult, however, must date to at least the tenth century because in 979 Queen Elfthryth founded a Benedictine monastery for women in Amesbury and dedicated it to St Melorus. The presence of his shrine may have been the reason why the queen chose the site.

There is a medieval life of St Melorus, abridged from a French work and probably written at Amesbury. It states that he was the son of Melianus, Duke of Cornouaille, in Brittany. When he was seven years old, his uncle Rivoldus murdered Melianus, seized his dukedom and, maiming St Melorus by cutting off his right hand and left foot, locked him away in a monastery, where he began to work miracles. This so alarmed his uncle that when the boy reached fourteen he persuaded St Melorus' guardian to behead him. The miracles continued. Many years afterwards, Breton missionaries brought the relics to Amesbury and placed them on the altar of the church. When they tried to remove them they adhered to the altar 'like adamant' so the relics remained in Wiltshire. Good's reference to Melorus' brother rather than uncle must be an error.

A S. Decumanus heremita ob Christi fidem decollatus caput suum ad
   fontem usque ubi id lauare solitus erat deportat

B S. Clarus sacerdos anglus dum Galliam pius peregrinus obit ob
   castimoniam seruatam interficitur.

C S. Iuthuuara uirgo impie occisa miracula edit.

PICTURE XIX

A.   St Decuman the hermit is beheaded for his faith in Christ, and takes his head to the spring where he was in the habit of washing it.

St Decuman was a sixth-century Welsh hermit from a noble family. Wanting solitude, he left his home of Rhoscrowther in Pembrokshire, crossed the Severn on a hurdle of reeds, and settled in north Somerset, near Dunster. A fifteenth-century *Life* states that he was decapitated while at prayer and his body carried his head to a nearby spring. This picture contains one of the most expressive faces in the wall paintings: a man in blue looks on in horror, his hair standing on end, as St Decuman walks past, with his blood-dripping head in his hands.

B.   St Clarus, an English priest, goes to France as a holy pilgrim, and is killed defending his chastity.

St Clarus was popular but the earliest surviving life of this probably eighth-century saint dates only from the twelfth century. Said to have been born in Rochester, he led an exemplary life, in word and deed, as a hermit in Normandy, eventually settling near Rouen. He received, however, the unwanted attentions of a noblewoman. He repulsed her and fled into a forest but the lady had two men hunt down St Clarus and behead him. The village of Saint-Clair-sur-Epte in the Île-de-France is named after him.

Bale had denigrated the cult of St Clarus, unhappy with another example of the English Church's engagement with the universal and papal

Church. William Good 'reinstated' the missionary hermit to counter this denigration.

St Juthwara, perhaps, was Cornish. Her relics were translated to Sherborne, Dorset, sometime between 1045 and 1058. Nothing else can be stated with certainty. Her late medieval legend is somewhat outlandish. According to this, as a young girl, St Juthwara prayed, fasted and gave alms. After her father's death she suffered pains in her chest; perhaps, because of her sorrow and austerities. Her wicked stepmother advised St Juthwara that she could cure herself of these

pains by applying cheese to her breast; at the same time she told her son that the girl was pregnant. St Juthwara's moist underclothes (from the cheese), seemed to confirm the pregnancy and the son decapitated the girl. The place of her death may have been Lanteglos by Camelford. After the decapitation, it is said that a spring of water appeared and St Juthwara carried her separated head to a church.

A S. Wenefredae Virgini ob uirginitatem a Cradoco Alani regis filio
   in Nort Wallia caput amputatur, eius capite in Vallem deuoluto
   fons erupit adhuc miraculis clarus.
B Cradocus a Daemone rapitur.
C Eiusdem Virginis capite à S. Benone corpori adiuncto ipsa ad
   quindecim annos superuixit.

PICTURE XX

A.   St Winefride, virgin, is beheaded in North Wales by Caradoc, son of King Alan, and her head rolls into the valley where a fountain springs up, and this is still famous for the miracles worked there.

B.   Caradoc is seized by the Devil.

C.   St Winefride's head is reattached to her body by St Beuno, and she lives a further fifteen years.

After St David, St Winefride is the most popular Welsh saint. She is the patroness of north Wales and her spring, Holywell, remains a place of pilgrimage. She died around 650 but the two surviving accounts of her life were written in the twelfth century. Robert, prior of Shrewsbury Monastery, wrote a *Life* to celebrate the translation of St Winefride's relics from Gwytherin to Shrewsbury in 1138. This is what we learn from his account: St Winefride's father was a wealthy man from Flintshire and her mother was the sister of the monk St Beuno, who settled near the family and inspired his niece by his life and preaching. A young man, Caradoc, a chieftain from Hawarden, fell in love with St Winefride and desired her but she would not satisfy his desires. One day, to get away from him, she fled to St Beuno's church but before she had reached it, Caradoc overtook her and, in his lecherous rage, cut off her head. Immediately, the young chieftain was swallowed up by the earth and, where St Winefride's head had fallen, a fountain sprang up. St Beuno, discovering his decapitated niece, brought her back to life by prayer and placing her head back on its shoulders, where it re-grew at once, leaving only a scar. St Winefride eventually left home and entered the convent of Gwytherin, where she became the abbess. Fifteen years after her miraculous resuscitation she died. Her relics remained at Gwytherin until their translation to Shrewsbury.

The cult of St Winefride was early and strong in north Wales but

the translation of her relics and the increasing accessibility of Holywell spread it further afield: in 1398 her feast was extended to the whole of southern England; in 1416, King Henry V made the pilgrimage on foot from Shrewsbury to Holywell; and the mother of King Henry VII, Lady Margaret Beaufort, built the fine chapel, which still stands at Holywell, after the Battle of Bosworth field. Holywell and its established reputation for cures were not diminished by the Reformation. There are plenty of accounts of large pilgrimages and healings in the seventeenth and eighteenth centuries. But even during the Elizabethan period, when persecution was most intense, Catholics visited Holywell. The English Jesuit and missionary to England, John Gerard, records of the spring water that it was 'extremely cold, but no one ever came to any harm by drinking it . . . I took several gulps of it myself on an empty stomach and nothing happened to me.' A

few years later, in the summer of 1605, another English Jesuit, Henry Garnet, in the company of leading Catholic laypeople, made a pilgrimage to Holywell for the sake of his health. When he was falsely tried for complicity in the Gunpowder Plot, it was said in court that the pilgrimage to the well 'was but a jargon, to have better opportunity, by colour thereof, to confer.'

We have seen many Welsh martyrs represented

in the wall paintings. This reflects the rich Catholic heritage of the country. Wales may have suffered the ignominy of being reduced to an administrative region of England by Parliament in 1536, but the English College honoured the land's saints. Was this a conscious act of healing? The first rector of the College had been a Welshman, Morus Clynnog, against whom the students had rebelled for his supposed partiality towards the Welsh students and, perhaps, because they disagreed on the purpose of this new institution. Pope Gregory XIII eventually dismissed Dr Clynnog and placed the Jesuits in charge. By giving plenty of wall space to the honouring of Welsh saints, William Good may have helped to sooth Welsh pride and remind the English students of Wales' contribution to the Church in Britain.

A S. Edouardus Angliae rex Alfridae nouercae insidiis transfoditur, ac
inter martyres colitur eiusque reliquiae magna in veneratione Glastoniae
habitae sunt.

B S. Elphegus Archiepūs Cantuariae post caedem crudelissimam sui
gregis a Danis infidelibus captiuus abducitur, multisque iniuriis affectus
securi cerebro impacta martyrii palmam obtinet.

PICTURE XXI

A.   St Edward, king of England is stabbed because of the plotting of his stepmother Elfrida. He is venerated among the martyrs. His relics are highly honoured at Glastonbury.

The first man who could call himself King of England was Egbert. In 825 he established supremacy over all other rulers. His descendents, however, were unable to maintain this supremacy and not for another hundred years, until Athelstan, could anyone claim to be King of the English. The newly designed coronation of Athelstan's descendent, Edgar, in 973 (though he had already been king for fifteen years) by St Dunstan, the Archbishop of Canterbury, was a powerful symbol of the king's authority and became the model for all subsequent coronations: a religious act, including anointing and crowning. King Edgar died only two years later, leaving two young heirs: the eldest St Edward, about thirteen years old, seems to have been fathered by Edgar before he was married, while Ethelred, who was no more than nine years old, and probably only six or seven, was the legitimate heir of Edgar by his marriage with Elfrida.

Neither boy was old enough, therefore, to argue their right to the crown; that was left to their elders. Queen Elfrida, of course, with others, including nobles and churchmen, supported Ethelred's claim but St Dunstan and Elfhere, the most powerful nobleman in the realm, supported St Edward's. So in 975, at Kingston-on-Thames, St Edward was crowned king. This, however, did not settle matters. For the next three years there was a state of near civil war and King Edward, still so young, was unable to make any impact on England north of the Thames.

The new king was kind to his stepmother and confirmed her former jurisdiction over the whole of Dorset. She established herself there, with her son, on a large estate centred on a natural mound dominating the gap of Corfe in the Purbeck hills. On 18 March 978, St Edward made a friendly visit to his half-brother. The Benedictine monk and scholar, Byrhtferth, writing at the beginning of the eleventh century recorded what happened: the king arrived in the early evening, accompanied by a small retinue. He was met at the gate of Elfrida's residence by her retainers, who dragged the king from his horse and murdered him. A hundred years later, William of Malmesbury added further details to the account of that fateful evening. These are depicted in Circignani's painting: while St Edward's attendants were seeing to his dogs, Elfrida, according to William, allured the king to her 'with female blandishment and made him lean forward, and after saluting him while he was eagerly drinking from the cup which had been presented, the dagger of an attendant pierced him through.' His body was hastily buried close by.

Nearly a year later, the nobleman Elfhere, who had supported St Edward, rode to Corfe and disinterred the body. He buried the remains, with great honour, at the convent of Shaftesbury. This was only possible after a year of negotiations between the different factions of the realm, which led to the coronation of Ethelred by St Dunstan on 4 May 979. The new king became one of the greatest supporters of his half-brother's cult. In 1001, he had the relics of St Edward the Martyr, translated to a richer shrine at Shaftesbury and made a grant in favour of the nuns, in which Ethelred stated, that this gift was being made to God and to 'his saint, my brother Edward, whom, drenched with his own blood, the Lord has seen fit to magnify in our time through many miracles.' Good, proud of his home town of Glastonbury, notes that some of St Edward's relics made their way there. King Ethelred himself fathered a future saint: St Edward the Confessor.

B.   St Alphege, Archbishop of Canterbury, sees his flock most cruelly massacred by the heathen Danes, and is then led away captive. He is very badly treated and eventually gains martyrdom by an axe cleaving his skull.

This is the first martyr in the wall paintings who died after the year 1000. St Alphege was a monk at Deerhurst in Gloucestershire but left to be a hermit in Somerset. St Dunstan made him Abbot of Bath and then, in 984, he became Bishop of Winchester. In 994, a Danish force led by Olav Tryggvason, harried the south of England. St Alphege was appointed by King Ethelred to officiate at the eventual peace treaty, in which England agreed to pay tribute to the Danes but, in return, Olaf promised to become a Christian and that he would never return 'with warlike intent'. In 1006, our former hermit completed his meteoric rise: the king chose him to be the Archbishop of Canterbury. St Alphege went to Rome himself to receive the pallium.

In 1011, the Danes returned and overran much of England. By September they had surrounded Canterbury and, after a fortnight's siege, they captured the city through the treachery of an Anglo-Saxon archdeacon. The archbishop was taken hostage and the Danes demanded £48,000 to be paid by the following Easter. The money was found but then more was demanded as a ransom for St Alphege, who, meanwhile, had been taken to Greenwich. The archbishop, however, would not allow this to be collected. On 19 April 1012, during a drunken feast, the Danes, angry with him, seized St Alphege and, according to the Anglo-Saxon Chronicle: 'shamefully put to death: they pelted him with bones and ox-heads, and one of them struck him on the head with the back of an axe, so that he sank down with the blow, and his holy blood fell on the ground, and so he sent his holy soul to God's kingdom.' St Alphege was immediately hailed a martyr and buried at St Paul's, London.

King Cnut, as he did with the other martyr who had suffered at the hands of the Danes, St Edmund, gave great honour to St Alphege. In 1023, he translated his relics to Canterbury, where they were buried to the north of the high altar. For some time after, the monks would venerate them at the beginning and end of each day. The discovery in 1105 that the body of St Alphege was incorrupt increased devotion to him and, following the rebuilding of the cathedral after the fire of 1174, a new stained-glass window was inserted to celebrate his life. After the Conquest, the new Archbishop of Canterbury, Lanfranc, with the usual Norman disdain towards Anglo-Saxon saints, questioned whether St Alphege was a true martyr. St Anselm, the Abbot of Bec and future Archbishop of Canterbury, defended the saint by arguing that as St John the Baptist was a martyr for truth, so St Alphege was a martyr for justice. In his last sermon, St Thomas of Canterbury alluded to his martyred predecessor and, just before his death, he commended his cause to God and St Alphege.

A S. Henricus Anglus Vpsaliae in Suetia Archiepiscopus, ab Adriano
P. P. IIII. Anglo Noruegiae Apostolo missus, finlandos conuertit:
inde Aboae archiepūs fidem Cristi Sanguine obsignat suo

B S. AEschillus Londae in Suetia Epūs, natione Anglus, saxis obruitur
Cantuaria. Angliae metropolis a Danis impiis capta incenditur, magna
Christianorum aedita caede in ipso templo Salvatoris nuncupato.

PICTURE XXII

A.   St Henry, an Englishman, Archbishop of Uppsala in Sweden, is sent by Pope Adrian IV (himself an Englishman) as apostle to Norway. He converts the Finns, and at Åbo bears testimony to his faith by shedding his blood.

In 1152, Pope Eugenius III sent the Englishman, Nicholas Breakspear (the future Pope Adrian IV), as his legate to Scandinavia. St Henry might have been part of the legate's retinue or one of those several Englishman who had been working as missionaries among the people of Sweden, the Svear and the Götar, from at least the early eleventh century. We cannot be absolutely sure, but it was probably on arriving in Sweden, at the council of Linköping, that Breakspear consecrated St Henry, Bishop of Uppsala. In 1154, provoked by Finnish expeditions into Sweden, King Eric IX, accompanied by the bishop, led a punitive response – entitled a crusade – against Finland. The king offered peace and the Christian faith to the Finns. They refused, the Swedes won the battle and St Henry baptised the defeated Finns at the spring of Kuppis near Åbo (now Turku).

King Eric returned home having created a union between Sweden and Finland that would last until the fourteenth century. St Henry remained behind and built a church at Nousis as a centre for missionary activity. He was martyred only a couple of years later in 1156 by a man called Lalli, a converted Finn, whom the bishop had excommunicated for murdering a Swedish soldier. Lalli, incensed with rage by St Henry's enforcement of the Church's penitential discipline, ambushed and killed him with an axe. St Henry was buried at Nousis; miracles followed. In 1296, Pope Boniface VIII allowed Åbo Cathedral to be dedicated to St Henry, the Apostle of Finland, and in 1300 his relics were translated there; they were removed by the Russians in 1720. St Henry was specially invoked in storms by the local seal-fishers.

It is a pity that Circignani incorrectly depicts the murderer, Lalli, holding a dagger over St Henry. In Nousis, for example, the town crest depicts the bishop sitting on a splendid Scandinavian chair, with his feet on a prostrate Lalli, who correctly clasps an axe.

B. St Eskil, Bishop of Lund in Sweden, English by nationality, is stoned to death.

About 830, St Anskar established a church at Birka, near Stockholm but this missionary centre did not survive and the local people relapsed into paganism. Then, during the reign of King Ethelred, Olav Trygvasson, King of Norway, requested missionaries from England. Ethelred dispatched St Sigfrid, a monk of Glastonbury, whose martyred nephews were depicted in Picture XI. St Eskil, a kinsman, accompanied him. The names Sigfrid and Eskil suggest Viking blood. It is thought that when Olav died, the missionaries went to Sweden where, at the beginning of the eleventh century, St Sigfrid baptised the Swedish King, Olav Skötkonung. St Eskil remained in Sweden, working principally in Södermanland and was ordained a bishop at Strängnäs, inland from what is now Stockholm.

In the years to come, St Eskil was supported by King Inge but some Swedes wanted to return to the Norse god. They murdered Inge and replaced him with the pagan Sweyn the Bloody. A festival to the old gods was held at Strängnäs. A pagan altar was built and sacrifices were prepared. St Eskil, seeing that Christians were taking part, confronted them and pleaded with them to desist. When they ignored him, St Eskil appealed to God for a visible sign that the God he preached was the true and only God. Immediately there was a hailstorm of such violence that it destroyed the altar and the sacrifices but spared St Eskil and his companions. Sweyn, ascribing this to magic, demanded that he should die so the crowd turned on St Eskil and stoned him to death. The recorded year of his martyrdom is around 1080. Until the Reformation,

St Eskil was honoured in northern Europe as one of the most illustrious martyrs of Scandinavia.

The details of St Eskil's life are based on two unsatisfactory medieval accounts. We can be confident that he was from England and became a missionary bishop in Sweden, who suffered martyrdom. The dates attributed to him, however, and the names of the Swedish kings with which he was supposedly connected are questionable. For example, if St Eskil did come to Scandinavia with St Sigfrid he would have been in his nineties when he was martyred. This is unlikely. Good notes that St Eskil was Bishop of Lund. This is an error. He is confusing him with a twelfth-century Eskil who became Archbishop of Lund.

The picture depicts, therefore, a late Anglo-Saxon Church in England, which is still sending out missionaries and is committed to its membership of the universal Church. Of course, for Bale, by the turn of the new millennium, the Catholic Church is completely the creature of the Antichrist.

B cont'd.   Canterbury, England's metropolitan city, is set on fire by the wicked Danes. There is great loss of life among the Christians, in the church dedicated to our Saviour.

The city of Canterbury was besieged by Danes in 1011. With the help of the traitorous Anglo-Saxon, Elfmaer, they broke into the city, pillaged it and set the cathedral on fire. Why did Good not place this scene in the previous picture (XXI) which includes St Alphege who was seized in the Danish attack upon Canterbury? Perhaps he wished to demonstrate that the efforts of Anglo-Saxon missionaries in Scandinavia had helped to rid England of danger from the north. Or was Good drawing a parallel in preparation for the next picture (XXIII)? As the Danes had despoiled Canterbury Cathedral and her shrines to such saints as Dunstan, so Henry VIII, a modern day Dane, had despoiled Canterbury's greatest shrine to England's most celebrated saint – St Thomas of Canterbury.

A   S. Thomas Archiepus Cantuariensis ab Henrico II Angliae rege inique
       damnatus ad Pont Max. appellat, fugamque init.

B   Coram Alexandro III Summo Pontifice Senone in Gallia causâ suâ agit

C   A regiis satellitibus pro ecclesiastica libertate occiditur anno 1171

D   Eius sanguis ac cerebrum in templi angulo proiecta fontem aquae
       producunt qui semel in lac, quater in cruorem uersus est.

Picture XXIII

A.   St Thomas, Archbishop of Canterbury, wrongly sentenced by King Henry II of England, appeals to the pope, and escapes.

B.   He pleads his cause before Pope Alexander III at Sens in France.

C.   He is murdered by the king's agents in 1171, for the freedom of the Church.

D.   His blood and his head, striking a corner of the church, cause a spring of water to flow, which turns once into a lake and four times into blood.

St Thomas was the first cockney to achieve high office in politics and the Church. Born in Cheapside, London, in 1120, into a prosperous Norman family, he received a good education but was probably more interested in rural sports. When his father ran into financial difficulties, he became a clerk to a banking house but, in 1145, he moved to the household of his kinsman Theobald, Archbishop of Canterbury. This launched his career. St Thomas was described at the time as tall and slender, with fair skin and dark hair. His forehead was wide, his eyes bright and his expression was considered calm and happy. He was vivacious and a charmer.

Theobald was quickly impressed by his new clerk and gave him important duties. St Thomas, in return, worked hard for his master and received further favours. Nine years later, in 1154, by the time he was thirty-four, St Thomas was well-established and rich with benefices. Then, in that year, Henry II came to the throne of England and by December, St Thomas was his chancellor. He may have been suggested to the king by the archbishop, who wanted the Church to have a man on the inside to support the Church's interests. The royal chancellorship was just another, albeit prestigious, clerkship but Henry and St Thomas became close friends. Through this friendship, St Thomas became a power at court and an influential councillor to the king.

On 18 April 1161, Archbishop Theobald died. At the time, St Thomas was commanding troops in a border war against King Louis

VII of France. Theobald had wanted his favourite clerk to succeed him. King Henry wanted this as well: he imagined a friendly and amenable archbishop who would support his plans for Church and State. St Thomas, however, was hesitant; he had enjoyed court life and he may have thought himself unsuitable. But the king got his way, with the help of the papal legate who overcame St Thomas' reluctance. On 2 June 1162, St Thomas was ordained a priest and the next day he was ordained bishop.

Very quickly, the relationship between the king and the new archbishop soured. On receiving the pallium from Rome, St Thomas resigned from the royal chancellorship as an office unsuitable to his ministry. This personally offended Henry; it seemed to him a snub. A year later, at a gathering in Woodstock, the king proposed that sheriff's aid, a traditional surcharge to the general land tax, should be diverted from the sheriffs to the royal treasury. St Thomas opposed such an idea and Henry, isolated and unused to being opposed, had to drop it. This was probably the moment when their relationship broke down irrevocably.

King Henry sought revenge in the area of law. Since the eleventh century, ecclesiastical reformers had striven to rid the Church of lay interference. For example, the Church in England had successfully exempted men in holy orders (benefit of clergy) from the jurisdiction of secular courts. This seemed outrageous to Henry: anyone, even in the most minor of holy orders, could commit murder but would not have to face the full force of the law as Church courts would not pass death sentences. Among other things, the king also disliked litigants appealing from English Church courts to the papal curial courts. At Westminster, in October 1163, aware that the archbishop had prevented several men in holy orders from being convicted in a lay court of a felony and so had safeguarded them from suffering the penalty of mutilation or death, Henry asked the assembled bishops to respect the ancient customs of the realm. They said they would 'saving their order'. This get-out clause, of course, did not resolve the issue.

Yet by the end of 1163, with the agreement of Pope Alexander III, St Thomas promised Henry that he would observe the customs of the realm as long as he only had to give a verbal assent to them. The king, however, summoned a great council to Woodstock in January 1154 and publicised the archbishop's assent as a royal victory. He

then browbeat St Thomas into a public declaration of assent and had drawn up the so-called Constitutions of Clarendon, which consisted of sixteen measures to curb the power of the Church courts and papal authority in England. The one that was most objectionable to St Thomas was the return of the practice that if a man in holy orders was convicted in a lay court of a serious crime, he would be released to the Church court to be stripped of his orders and then returned as a layman to the secular authorities to receive his punishment under secular law. The bishops managed not to sign the constitutions but St Thomas judged that he had sinned by giving his verbal assent. He suspended himself from priestly duties, imposed penance on himself and wrote to the pope.

The king had not yet finished with his archbishop. In October, St Thomas, as depicted in the painting, was summoned to Northampton Castle to attend a council of the magnates. He was accused of denying justice in the feudal court to the baron John Marshal, from whom he had taken back lands belonging to Canterbury. The charge did not stick but then the king accused St Thomas of the embezzlement of royal revenues while serving as chancellor. When Henry refused the bishop of Winchester's offer to pay a fine to settle the matter, St Thomas feared that the king wished him grave harm. On 13 October, before the Bishops could declare the court's judgement on him, the archbishop appealed to the pope. Henry made a counter-appeal and added St Thomas' appeal to the list of his crimes, since it was judged to be in breach of the Constitutions of Clarendon. When the chief justiciar approached him, St Thomas refused to hear the judgement – barons were incompetent to judge an archbishop – marched out of the room, slipped out of the castle and escaped to France.

Orlando Bandinelli had been elected pope in September 1159, taking the name Alexander III. A few cardinals, loyal to the interests of the Holy Roman Emperor, Frederick I Barbarossa, opposed his election and chose someone else for the papacy, the antipope, Victor IV. This schism would last for eighteen years, with Victor IV being succeeded by two more antipopes. Alexander III, however, had the support of the Kings of England and France. Faced with imperial opposition in Italy, Pope Alexander moved to France and from 1163 to 1165 settled with the curia at Sens. There St Thomas presented himself to the pope. He produced a copy of the Constitutions of Clarendon and took Alexander through them clause by clause. Mindful that he must not alienate Henry II, one of his supporters, the pope declared that though none of the laws were good and some were directly contrary to canon law, others were tolerable, and then took care not to write down these opinions. Having done all he could, St Thomas retired to the Cistercian abbey at Pontigny and waited.

By the end of 1165, Alexander III had been able to return to Rome and so, feeling more secure, gave St Thomas legatine powers. Visiting the Cluniac abbey of Vézelay for Whitsunday 1166, the archbishop celebrated the public Mass and shared with the congregation his wrongs and sufferings. And then, with his legatine powers, he condemned the Constitutions of Clarendon and those who supported them and passed sentences of anathema and excommunication on all the royal servants who had acted against him. He stopped short, however, at naming the king. Hearing of this, Henry had the bishops of his realm appeal to the pope. In November, St Thomas and his supporters moved from their residence at Pontigny to the preferable location of the Benedictine abbey of St Columba outside the city of Sens. There they remained for the next four years. During this time the penitential life, which St Thomas had adopted at his ordination, grew more severe: he wore a hair shirt and had his chaplain scourge his back daily.

Pope Alexander worked hard for reconciliation between king and archbishop. By 1169, Henry had made many concessions, including the scrutiny of certain laws, and the abatement of some of the financial claims he had made against St Thomas at Northampton. St Thomas, however, distrusted the king, fearing that once he had returned to Henry's dominions, he would be arrested. He repeatedly demanded, therefore, a kiss of peace from Henry. Then, in the summer of 1170, the King had his heir, the young Henry, crowned King of England by the Archbishop of York and ten other bishops. The king's concern was to ensure a smooth succession. St Thomas, however, saw this as a usurpation of his authority as Archbishop of Canterbury and he wrongly believed that young Henry had sworn to uphold the Constitutions of Clarendon.

A peace, however, was finally patched up and, on 22 July 1170 at Fréteval, the king and archbishop met on horseback and settled their differences. Some excommunications of royal officials remained but St Thomas explained that he was unable to lift them because they had been imposed by the pope. On 2 December, after an exile of six years, the archbishop returned to his cathedral. Any jubilation was short lived. Ranulf de Broc, a royal servant who had had custody of the temporalities of Canterbury during the exile and taken much for himself, blockaded the city and, on Christmas Day St Thomas publicly announced the papal excommunications of those bishops who had been involved in the coronation of the younger Henry. Some of these prelates had already travelled to Henry's Christmas court at Bur-le-Roi, near Bayeux. They blamed St Thomas for all the disagreements and accused him of breaking the peace. It was probably on Christmas Day, as St Thomas celebrated the Nativity in Canterbury Cathedral, that King Henry said to those around him those fateful words: 'What miserable drones and traitors have I nurtured and promoted in my household who let their lord be treated with such shameful contempt by a low-born clerk.'

Four of Henry's knights – William de Tracey, Reginald Fitzurse, Hugh de Morville and Richard Brito – spurred into action by the king's words, immediately left the royal court and sailed for England. A few days later they gathered at Saltwood Castle in Kent, held by Ranulf de Broc, and formulated their plan: they would confront the archbishop, make him absolve the bishops and receive his pledges of good behaviour. The next day, during the wintry afternoon of 29 December, they were permitted to enter St Thomas' chamber at Canterbury. He did not rise to greet them or end his conversation with a monk. Angry exchanges followed but before the knights could act the chamber was filled with members of the archbishop's household. The soldiers left for reinforcements and his clerks forced St Thomas into the asylum of the cathedral. He refused their request, however, for the doors of the cathedral to be bolted and waited for the anticipated knights in the centre of the opening to the north transept. What happened next is the most documented event of the twelfth century; we have a number of eyewitness accounts.

All his clerks had by now deserted St Thomas, except for a visitor, Edward Grim, depicted in the painting holding the archiepiscopal cross. The monks, who had been celebrating vespers in the choir, watched from a safe distance. Entering the cathedral with their swords drawn, the knights cried out, 'Where is Thomas Becket, traitor to the king and the kingdom?' St Thomas replied, 'Here I am, no traitor to the king, but a priest. What do you want from me?' The knights demanded that the excommunications be lifted but St Thomas said that was impossible until satisfaction had been made. 'Then,' the knights said, 'you will now die and get what you deserve.' The archbishop replied, 'I am prepared to die for my Lord so that in my blood the Church may find liberty and peace, but I forbid you in the name of Almighty God to harm my men, whether clerk or lay, in any way.' The knights then tried to drag him outside the cathedral but he could not be budged. So, all of a sudden, one knight struck with his sword, cutting off the top of the archbishop's crown. Despite this, St Thomas remained standing. Then another knight struck but still St Thomas stood. At the third sword blow, however, he fell and said in a low voice, 'For the name of Jesus and the well-being of the Church I am prepared to embrace death.' More blows followed until the archbishop was, without a doubt, dead. One knight put his foot on St Thomas's neck and, with the point of his sword, scattered the brains. 'Let us go, knights,' he called out to the others, 'this fellow will not get up again.'

The archbishop's body was left unburied until the next day, when a kinsman of Ranulf de Broc ordered it to be buried in an obscure corner. Placing it in a marble sarcophagus, prepared for another burial, the body was sunk into the floor of the Trinity Chapel at the eastern end of the crypt. The public horror at the news of St Thomas' death was great and, despite his protestations of innocence, Henry II was held responsible. And then the miracles began. The first known miraculous cure was in Canterbury on 4 January 1171; over the next ten years 703 more were recorded. Some of the earliest cures followed the drinking of small amounts of St Thomas' blood, which had been scraped from the cathedral floor, and diluted in water. By Easter 1171, John of Salisbury, a colleague and friend of St Thomas for fifteen years, was able to write that 'both in the place of his passion and before the high altar, where he spent the night before burial, and at the place of burial, the paralyzed are cured, the blind see, the deaf hear, the mute speak, the crippled walk, the fevered are relieved, the possessed are freed from the devil, and the sick are cured from diverse illnesses.'

On 21 February 1173, Pope Alexander III canonised Archbishop Thomas and the next year, in June, King Henry II made a penitential pilgrimage to Canterbury, walking the last mile barefoot and accepting a scourging at the hands of the monks. In 1220, after various political delays, St Thomas' body was translated to a purpose-built shrine. This became the most popular pilgrimage destination in England and one of the most popular in Europe. Soon the windows of the cathedral were decorated with glass celebrating the miracles of the great saint and, throughout Christendom, St Thomas was held up as a model bishop.

Three hundred years later, King Henry VIII rejected papal authority, then the independence of the priesthood, then monasticism and, finally, the cult of the saints. St Thomas, therefore, became the least acceptable of all the saints of England. His appeal to Pope Alexander was considered treason, his defence of clerical immunity was unlawful protection of criminals, his monastic connections confirmed his attachment to foreign powers, and his supposed status as a martyr and saint concealed his real betrayal of England. In November 1538, King Henry issued a proclamation designed to destroy the memory of St Thomas. His shrine had already been pillaged and his bones scattered in early September. Described as a rebel to his king and supporter of papal abuses, he was no longer to be considered a saint and his images and pictures were to 'be put down and avoided out of all churches, chapels and other places.' His name was to be scratched out from all liturgical books and his Office, antiphons and collects to be said no more. By abolishing his feast days, it was said that 'his grace's loving subjects shall be no longer blindly led and abused to commit idolatry.'

In his work *The Actes of Englysh votaryes*, Bale begins his account of St Thomas with the heading 'the freshe and lusty begynnynges of Thomas Becket', claiming that his early life had been one of debauchery, despite the complete consensus of contemporaries that he had remained chaste, notwithstanding life at court. Bale's description of St Thomas' death is completely unsympathetic and includes an attack against invocations to saints: the knights had 'pared his plyde crowne with theyr swerdes, and cut of the popes marke to hys very braine whyls he in ydolatry com[m]ended himself and the cause of hys churche to hys patrone S Denyse, beynge but a deade ymage there standing upon the aultre.' St Thomas' murder was not, according to Bale, the death of a martyr but of a traitor and his canonisation was papal endorsement of such treason: 'thus ended he his lyfe in most ranke treaso[n] & was for his labour made a god of ye papistes.' The miracles attributed to St Thomas were attacked in particular by Bale's protégée, Foxe: 'If they were true, [the miracles] were wrought not by God, but by a contrary spirit; . . . or else . . . fayned and forged of idle Monks and religious bellies, for the exaltation of their churches, and profit of their powches.'

In 1586, after nearly fifty years of scorn poured upon St Thomas' memory, the chronicler, Raphael Holinshed, mocked those who still venerated him as a saint: 'what remembrance is there now of Thomas Becket? Where be the shrines that were erected in this church and that chapel for perpetuities of his name and fame? . . . And although the pope ment by causing such ikons to be erected to prefer Thomas as a perpetual saint to all posterities . . . yet is he growne not all to renowne but infamie and shame in England.' Yet at that time in Rome, in the English College dedicated to St Thomas, as had been the Hospice, students prayed before an altarpiece – the Martyrs' Picture – which depicted him and on their church wall they honoured him. His example inspired them to return to England to exercise their priestly ministry, despite the possible consequences.

St Thomas remained important to all English and Welsh Catholics. His willingness to oppose the king in defence of the church was an inspiration to them. Fifty years before the wall paintings, on the eve of his own execution, in his last letter to his daughter Meg, St Thomas More had written: 'I cumber you, good Margaret, much, but I would be sorry if it [the execution] should be any longer than tomorrow, for it is St Thomas' Even and the Utas [octave] of St Peter, and therefore tomorrow long I to go to God – it were a day very meet and convenient for me.' As Thomas Stapleton noted in his 1588 work *Tres Thomae*, both St Thomases had died for the primacy of the papacy, without which 'a way is opened to all the heresies, and the wolves ravage the flock with impunity.'

The *South English Legendary*, compiled sometime in the late twelfth century, in its description of St Thomas' death, emphasises the blood and brain that flowed from the wounds of his head. Circignani's picture illustrates this and reminds us of the ancient church teaching that the blood of the martyrs is the seed of Christians. Now, however, the wall paintings are about to consider a new type of martyr; one who dies entirely for church unity and the authority of the papacy. St Thomas is a hinge between them and the earliest martyrs of the Church.

A | S. Gulielmus puer Nordouici in Anglia eodem mortis genere quò Christus
   a Judæis in festo Paschalis ad fidei nostræ contumeliam occiditur.
B | S. Hugo puer Lincolniæ eodem modo a Judæis crucifigitur
C | S. Thomas monachus Dounæ à Gallis occisus post mortem
   miraculis coruscat.

PICTURE XXIV

A. St William, a child of Norwich in England, suffered the same death as Christ by the Jews, at the feast of the Passover, in contempt of our holy faith.

B. St Hugh, a boy of Lincoln, is similarly crucified by the Jews.

This is a most unfortunate picture. The cults of these two boy 'saints' reflect medieval England's anti-Semitism.

In 1144, the body of a twelve year old called William was found on Easter Monday in a wood outside Norwich. Two days after the discovery, the boy's uncle, a priest called Godwin, accused the Jewish community of Norwich of his nephew's ritualistic murder. Any further details about William come from a *Life*, written around 1169, by Thomas of Monmouth, who became the sacristan of the boy's shrine. According to this, William was apprenticed to a skinner and because of his master's work came into frequent contact with the Jewish community. During Holy Week, tricked into accompanying a stranger who promised him a new job, the boy was taken to a Jew's house where he was gagged, shaved, crowned with thorns and crucified. Thomas got these details, some years after William's death, from Theobald, a converted Jew of Cambridge, who claimed that once a year, the Jewish People would sacrifice a victim, choosing, every time, a different country and city.

Bishop Everard of Norwich did not believe Godwin's accusation, and the sheriff of Norwich defended the Jewish community, taking them into the castle for their protection. The prior of Norwich Cathedral, William Turbe, however, believed from the first that the Jews had murdered the boy. He worked hard to promote a cult to William, which became easier when he was elected Bishop of Norwich in 1146. After the boy's body was removed from its original burial place in the wood, it was shifted from tomb to tomb within the chapterhouse in Norwich until its final enshrinement in 1154 on the north side of the rood screen. At first the shrine was popular but, by 1314, the offerings at the shrine were only

£1 1s. 5d. and, by 1343, they were worth a mere 4d. Long before the Reformation, devotion to the 'saint and martyr of Norwich' had waned.

Godwin's accusation and Theobald's 'explanation' made William's death the first alleged victim of Jewish ritual murder in England, and indeed in Europe. Sadly, it was not the last. In 1255, the body of a nine-year-old boy called Hugh was found in Lincoln in a well inside the house of Copin, a Jew; what was most likely an accident was immediately described as a ritual murder. Threatened with torture and death, Copin confessed and implicated all other Jews in the realm, stating that 'nearly all the Jews in England agreed to the death of this boy,' which involved scourging, crowning with thorns, and crucifixion. Despite promises to the contrary, Copin was executed on the orders of King Henry III: he was tied to a horse's tail and dragged up and down the steep streets of Lincoln and then hanged. One hundred other implicated Jews were taken to London, where eighteen were executed. The others were eventually released but only after paying a large fine. Hugh's body was buried in Lincoln Cathedral and his story was memorialised through the Prioress's Tale in Chaucer's *Canterbury Tales*.

The first recorded Jews in England had arrived after the Norman Conquest. Until their expulsion from the realm (the first kingdom ever to do such a thing) in 1290, they were continually persecuted. Why did they not leave? The crown would not give them permission to do so, considering the Jews to be a royal milch-cow, from which money could be demanded at will. It is to our shame that the nonsensical belief in Jewish ritual murder began in England. The Church vigorously refuted the notion – in the thirteenth century both Pope Innocent IV and Pope Gregory X defended the innocence of the Jews – but local persecutions still occurred.

Neither William nor Hugh was canonised. Their popularity was ephemeral; the alleged cause of their deaths denied by the universal Church. However, Good included them because Bale (rightly) had dismissed them and because, as children, they alluded to other (real) martyrs: the Holy Innocents. These infant saints were a common representation in art for martyrs in general. The Roman Breviary stated for their feast day:

> These then, whom Herod's cruelty tore as sucklings from their mother's bosom, are justly hailed as "infant Martyr flowers"; they were the Church's first blossoms, matured by the frost of persecution during the cold winter of belief.'

In the wall paintings of San Stefano Rotondo, Circignani included the Holy Innocents in the crucifixion scene as the representative martyrs venerating Christ's death. In the English College's wall paintings, Hugh and William are our Holy Innocents, purposefully depicted in the last of the twenty-four pictures, which completes the history of the Church in England and Wales before the Reformation. The two boys are an unfortunate summary of all that has gone before, and they connect us to what will come: the Catholic martyrs of the sixteenth-century Church.

C.   St Thomas, a monk of Douai, is killed by the French, and is renowned for the miracles he works after his death.

St Thomas was a Benedictine monk of the priory of St Martin at Dover (mistakenly referred to by Good as Douai), a cell of the monastery at Canterbury, who was killed during a French raid on 2 August 1295. According to a *Life*, written shortly after his death, when the raid began the monks fled, except for St Thomas who, in accordance with the Benedictine Rule, went to take his midday siesta. The French, guided by men from Calais, entered the priory, found St Thomas in the dormitory and demanded that he show them where the chalices and charters were kept. When he refused, they killed him. St Thomas was buried in the priory church and his grave became a locally popular place for pilgrimage. Eighty years later, Pope Urban VI set up a commission to study his life and death, having been petitioned by King Richard II and 'several noble Englishman' to canonise him. Meanwhile, indulgences were given for visiting the grave. Nothing ever came of the commission and St Thomas was never actually canonised.

A Ioannes Fischerus. ep̄s Roffensis in Anglia Card. declaratus, vitae et doctrinae
  integerr. laude clariss. ab Henr. VIII. quod Pont. auc̄tem tueretur capite plectitur.
B Thomas Morus, eques auratus, summo regni maḡratu perfunctus, prudentia, eruditione,
  morum innocentia et suauitate insignis, ob eandem causam eiusdem Regis iussu securi
  percutitur. Ambo Anglicanae reipub. lumina, alter sacri, alter laici ordinis decus.
C Margarita regiae familiae foemina prudentiss. Comitissa Sar. Card. Poli m̄r.
  ob gestam̄ insigne quinq. plagar. Christi, eadem morte, sub eodem Rege, plexa est.

PICTURE XXV

A.   John Fisher, Bishop of Rochester in England, is made a cardinal. He is a man of exemplary life and teaching, and universally praised. He is beheaded by King Henry VIII for defending the authority of the pope.

St John Fisher was a man of great sanctity and learning. He was born at Beverley in 1469. At Cambridge he had a brilliant academic career, became a priest and by 1501 was vice-chancellor of the University. In the mid-1490s, St John had met Lady Margaret Beaufort, the mother of King Henry VII. She was immensely impressed by him and, in 1502, he resigned the vice-chancellorship to be her chaplain, but, in 1504 he was made chancellor of the university and Bishop of Rochester, a poor and small see (normally reserved for theologians), which he tended with great care. With his guidance, Lady Beaufort became a great patron of Cambridge and her money enabled St John to encourage the newest learning, including the study of Hebrew and Greek. Famed as a preacher, he was the panegyrist in 1509 at the funerals of both the king and his mother.

Throughout the 1520s, St John proved himself an able opponent of Martin Luther, producing a number of works against the reformer's writings. Then, in 1527 he was drawn into 'the King's Great Matter'. Henry VIII sought his opinion about the validity of his marriage to Katherine of Aragon. St John Fisher, unaware of what the king wished

177

to hear, defended the marriage, thinking that he was allaying the king's fears. As he grew in awareness of Henry's real intentions, his vocal support of Queen Katherine increased and he said of himself that he had never studied any other matter more closely than the validity of the royal marriage. When, in 1529, a tribunal at the London Blackfriars failed to resolve the issue and Queen Katherine had swept out of the hall, St John told those assembled that he was willing to die for the sanctity of the marriage bond and he likened himself to St John the Baptist. This, of course, made the king and Anne Boleyn, Herod and Herodias.

For the next six years, until his death, St John was Henry VIII's most consistent opponent. This led someone – not the king – to have the bishop's soup poisoned but, because of his asceticism, he had given the entire meal to his servants and the poor at his gates. Two of them were killed and the rest left seriously ill. After a number of political and legal close shaves, St John was finally cornered in April 1534 by his unwillingness to take the 'Oath of Succession', which was required of all adult males. That Parliament could decide the line of succession, he acknowledged, but the oath's preamble went further and rejected papal authority. His refusal to take the oath led to his confinement in the Tower of London. By the end of the year he had been stripped of his preferments, including Rochester.

In May 1535, Pope Paul III raised St John to the College of Cardinals. This may have been an attempt to save him but was also recognition of his theological ability, which the pope hoped to use at the proposed Council of the Church but, as the king quipped, St John would not have a head upon which to wear his new hat. Having denied, in his cell, Henry's status as 'Supreme Head of the Church of England', which had been recognised by Act of Parliament in late 1534, and denial of which had been made treasonable by a new Act of Parliament in early 1535, St John was sentenced to death on 17 June. Five days later, at five o'clock in the morning, he was woken to be told that he would die that day. Very weak from his long struggles and imprisonment, he was carried in a chair to Tower Hill but walked unassisted up the steps to the scaffold. He pardoned his executioner and addressed the crowd telling them that he was dying for the faith of Christ's holy Catholic Church. He then asked them to pray for him that he might be steadfast to the end. After reciting the *Te Deum* and the psalm *In te Domine speravi* ('In you, O Lord, I take refuge'), he knelt down and the axe fell. St John Fisher remains the only cardinal who has died for the Catholic faith.

B.   Thomas More, a revered knight, performs the highest office in the land, and is renowned for his prudence, erudition, virtuous life and sweetness of character. He is beheaded with an axe by the same king for the same reason. Both these men are inspiring lights for the English nation, the first adorning the clerical, the second the lay state.

Like St John, in April 1534, St Thomas More was confined to the Tower of London. He also had refused to take the Oath of Succession because of its rejection of papal authority. St Thomas, however, did not share with anyone else his thinking upon the matter but maintained a studious silence at all times upon such issues. His silence was his best defence as it implied consent. He was visited many times in the Tower by the king's councillors, including Thomas Cromwell, who tried to browbeat him into submission but he did not bend; rather he wrote two masterpieces. In a Latin work, *De Tristitia Christi*, he meditated upon Christ's agony in the garden, the sleep of the disciples and the betrayal by Judas. His other work, *A Dialogue of Comfort Against Tribulation* is set in Hungary in 1528, as the country expected another attack from Suleiman the Magnificent. The work is ostensibly an encouragement to Hungarians who would soon suffer under Turkish rule. The analogy to England's own situation is clear. St Thomas, who reasonably had sought to live, was now preparing to die.

St Thomas was put on trial on 1 July 1535. He was found guilty of the offence of high treason, having allegedly rejected three weeks before in his cell, the King's title of Supreme Head of the Church of England in the presence of the Solicitor General, Richard Rich. St Thomas had not done such a thing; Rich had perjured himself. But now that he had been found guilty, St Thomas spoke his mind:

> Seeing that I see ye are determined to condemne me (God knoweth howe) I will nowe in discharge of my conscience speake my minde plainlye and freely touching my Inditment and your Statute withal. Forasmuch as, my Lorde, this Indictment is grounded uppon an acte of parliament directly repugnant to the lawes of god and his holy churche, the supreeme gouerment of which, or of any parte whereof, may no temporall prince presume by any lawe to take uppon him, as rightfully belonging to the See of Rome, a spirituall preheminence by the mouth of our Sauiour himself, personally present upon the earth, only to St Peter and his successors, Byshopps of the same See, by speciall prerogative graunted; It is therefore in lawe amongst Christen men insufficient to charge any Christen man. This Realme, being but one member and smale parte of the Church, might not make a particular lawe disagreeable with the generall lawe of Christes universall Catholike Churche. No more than the city of London, being but one poore member in respect of the whole realme, might make a lawe against an acte of parliament to bind the whole realme. No more might this realme of England refuse obediens to the Sea of Rome then might a child refuse obediens to his owne naturall father.

St Thomas was executed on Tower Hill on 6 July, the feast of the translation of the relics of St Thomas of Canterbury. Obedient to the king's final request of him that he speak briefly, a contemporary account records that St Thomas only 'asked the bystanders to pray for him in this world, and he would pray for them elsewhere. He then begged them earnestly to pray for the king, that it might please God to give him good counsel, protesting that he died the king's good servant but God's first.' St Thomas then turned to his executioner, kissed him and said: 'Thou wilt give me this day a greater benefit than ever any mortal man can be able to give me. Pluck up thy spirits, man, and be not afraid to do thine office. My neck is very short: take heed, therefore, thou strike not awry for saving of thine honesty.' St Thomas then covered his face with a linen cloth he had carried with him and was killed with one stroke.

Picture XXV is the beginning of the second group within the

wall paintings. Its ten pictures depict the Catholic martyrs of Tudor England. For the students in 1583, looking back to the events of 1535 is comparable to us regarding the Cuban Missile Crisis or the assassination of President Kennedy; it was a different world yet still familiar. The unbroken painted connection between the deaths of Fisher and More and all those that had gone before is Good's principal point: those who died for the faith of the Church under Henry and since, are no less martyrs than St Oswald, St Winefride or St Thomas of Canterbury; as St John said at Tower Hill: he was dying for the faith of Christ's holy Catholic Church.

Within a year of their deaths, Reginald Pole had established in his work *De Unitate* the importance of the witness of Fisher and More. Addressing King Henry VIII, Pole wrote of the two men that God 'has sent us [as] books against your deceitful wisdom . . . we have these writings from the finger of God, the very holy martyrs of God . . . a certain book written not with ink but with blood.' When he became the Archbishop of Canterbury, Cardinal Pole encouraged the continued use of St John and St Thomas as examples. Nicholas Harpsfield, the Archdeacon of Canterbury, wrote of St John Fisher, 'whose singuler virtue all Inglande well knewe, and whose singuler deepe knowledge in divinitie all the world knew as well as the Protestantes.' These words come from his *Life of More*, which, though it was not published during the author's time, spread widely in manuscript form. Harpsfield describes St Thomas as 'our blessed Protomartyr of all the laity for the preservation of the unitie of Christes Churche.' Good alludes to this description of More in his annotation to this picture. Harpsfield, however, went even further in his glorification of the former lord chancellor. He describes his martyrdom as more important than St Thomas of Canterbury's because, while the archbishop had died for objecting to any reduction of papal authority, More had died in defence of papal authority itself.

It is worth noting that for the rest of the wall paintings, there are no references to miracles. While the miracles of England and Wales' early martyrs demonstrated that they were founding the true Church among pagans, the lack of miracles associated with the Catholic Tudor martyrs demonstrated, despite reformers' protestations, that the true Church had been established – the Catholic Church – and Fisher, More and the others died witnessing to it.

Blessed Margaret Pole, the Countess of Salisbury and the mother of Cardinal Pole, is the only woman depicted in this last group of pictures. She is shown on the same scaffold as St John and St Thomas but she was not executed until 27 May 1541. Her walk to the scaffold, however, had begun many years before.

Bl. Margaret first angered Henry VIII by her support of Queen Katherine and Princess Mary. This made her unwelcome at court. She was received back into the king's favour, if not his love, after the fall of Anne Boleyn but was suspected again after the arrival in England of her son's work, *De Unitate*. Her death was procured by the false allegation in 1538 that she had been involved in the imagined Exeter Conspiracy. During interrogation she demonstrated that she was the niece of two kings, refusing to be cowed by threats. The Earl of Southampton said of her 'we suppose, that there hath not been seen or her[d of a] woman, so earnest in her co[untenance] manlique in continuance and . . . so precise aswell in gest[ure or in] words, that wonder is to be.' At first Bl. Margaret was kept under house arrest but by November 1539 she was confined in the Tower. Rather than bring her to trial, she was condemned to death by an Act of Attainder which had been passed through Parliament earlier in the year. The Act stated that she had aided and abetted her sons Henry and Reginald and had 'comytted and p[er]petrated div[er]se and sundrie other detestable and abhomynable treasons.' To prove this completely false allegation to the House of Lords, Thomas Cromwell produced a coat of armour, decorated with the five wounds of Christ (the symbol of the Pilgrimage of Grace, a Catholic uprising in 1536), which was allegedly found among Bl. Margaret's possessions, and which, it was said, symbolised Reginald Pole's intention to marry the Princess Mary and restore papal authority.

Early in the morning of 27 May 1541, two years after the Act of Attainder had been passed and one and a half years after entering the Tower – without any previous warning – Bl. Margaret was told that she was to die within the hour. Only a small crowd awaited her when the sixty-seven year-old woman was led out to East Smithfied Green, within the precincts of the Tower, where, not a scaffold, but a low block had been prepared. She took time to pray for the Royal Family and asked to be especially remembered to Princess Mary. Unfortunately, Bl. Margaret's death was not easy. According to Chapuys, the Spanish ambassador to Henry's court, the regular executioner was not available so 'a wretched and blundering youth had been chosen to take his place, who literally hacked her head and shoulders to pieces in the most pitiful manner.'

A Pro primatu Sancti Petri, eiusq. successorum in Sancta Romana ecclesia septem
   Angli Carthusiani monachi saeve laniati sunt.
B Novem alii eius ordinis carceris paedore et fame enecti. Cum primis passi
   sunt Reginaldus ordinis S. Brigittae, Ioānes Haulus sacerdos
C Duo alii Carthusiani Eboraci catenis ferreis e sublimi trabe vivi pendent,
   donec ossibus dissolutis dilabuntur et complures alii alias eam ob rem
   dilacerantur, Henrico VIII. Angliae rege iubente Anno M.D.X.X.X.V.

PICTURE XXVI

A.   Seven English Carthusian monks are savagely torn to pieces for the primacy of St Peter and his successors in the Holy Roman Church.

B.   Nine other members of the same Order die from exhaustion by filth and hunger. Along with the first, Reynolds of the Order of St Bridget, and John Haile, a priest, also suffer.

C.   At York, two other Carthusians hang in iron chains, while still alive, from a high beam, until their bones give way and they fall apart. Many others, in other places, are savagely done to death at the command of Henry VIII, in the year 1535.

Within their cloister, the outside world and its business must have seemed far away to the Carthusians of the London Charterhouse. Their days were a round of prayer, work and study. But in May 1534, the outside world broke in when the royal commissioners arrived to obtain oaths to the Act of Succession. The prior of the house, St John Houghton, asked whether the community should be exempted from the oath, since they were not concerned with worldly affairs. The commissioners' response was to arrest St John and his procurator, Bl. Humphrey Middlemore, and send them to the Tower. By the end of the month, however, the Bishop of London and others had persuaded the two monks that the oath was consistent with the Catholic faith and so with the added proviso, 'as far as the law of God permits', they took it and were released. The rest of the community only took the oath after much consideration, with the same proviso and with armed guards standing over them.

Then, in late 1534, Parliament passed the Act of Supremacy, which declared that the king was the Supreme Head of the Church of England and, in early 1535, it passed another Act which made it high treason to deny the king this title. When news of these developments reached the London Charterhouse, St John gathered the community to the chapter house and warned them that they would soon have to make a choice between death and apostasy. He then introduced three special days of preparation for the inevitable confrontation. On the first day the Carthusians made a general confession to each other; on the second, St John spoke to them of love and patience ending with the words, 'It is better for us to undergo a short suffering here for our sins, than to lay up for ourselves eternal torments'; on the third day, the community celebrated a solemn Votive Mass of the Holy Spirit to acquire the graces they would need.

St John then decided to make a personal appeal to Thomas Cromwell, hoping to gain an exemption from the new oath or, at least, a mitigation of it. He took with him two other priors who had come to consult with him: St Robert Lawrence of Beauvale and St Augustine Webster of the Isle of Axholme. They were allowed to see Cromwell but, having hardly spoken, all three were arrested and sent to the Tower. They were soon joined by a Bridgettine monk from Syon, St Richard Reynolds, who had also queried the oath. The prisoners said to Cromwell, when he once visited them, that they would take the oath if they could add the proviso, 'as far as the law of God allows'. The king's secretary replied, 'I admit of no condition. Whether the law of God permits or not, you must take the oath without reservation.' On 29 April 1535, the four monks were condemned of high treason for denying that Henry was the Supreme Head of the Church in England. A secular priest, Blessed John Haile, was also sentenced with them for speaking against the king, the queen and the royal council.

On 4 May the four monks, in their habits, and Bl. John were dragged

to Tyburn, lying on their backs on hurdles. St Thomas More, from his cell window, saw them leaving the Tower and said to his daughter standing beside him: 'Lo, dost thou not see, Meg, that these blessed Fathers be now as cheerfully going to their deaths, as bridegrooms to their marriage.' St John Houghton was executed first. As he was standing on the ladder, waiting to be hanged, he addressed the assembled thousands: 'I call God to witness, and beg of you all likewise to bear me witness at the dread judgement day, that here, about to die, I declare publicly that I refuse to comply with the will of our Lord the King, not out of any pertinacity, malice, or rebellious disposition, but only from the fear of God, lest I should offend His Sovereign Majesty, seeing our holy Mother the Church has decreed and determined otherwise than the king and his Parliament has ordained; wherefore I am obliged, in conscience, and am also ready and not dismayed, to suffer these and all possible torments rather than oppose the teaching of the Church. Pray for me, and pity my brethren whose unworthy prior I have been.' He was then turned off the ladder but was hardly allowed to hang when he was cut down and, while fully conscious, cut open. When the executioner went to tear out his heart, St John, spoke for the last time, asking: 'Good Jesus, what will ye do with my heart?' The rest of his companions then shared the same barbarous end. St Richard Reynolds was the last to be executed, having had to witness the deaths of the others. A year later, Pole referred to him in *De Unitate*:

> One of these martyrs I must not pass over without a special notice, as he was intimately known to me. Reynolds was his name, and he was one who, for the sanctity of his life, might be compared with the very first of those who profess the more exact rule of conduct according to the discipline of Christ, and had moreover, which is a thing seldom found in those who follow that profession, a more than common knowledge of all the liberal arts, a knowledge too, derived from the original sources. He was well acquainted with the three chief languages, in which all liberal learning is comprised, and, of all the monks in England, was the only one who had this knowledge. To manifest to all future time the praises of his sanctity and doctrine, and to show the height of his piety to Christ and his charity towards his country, one thing only seemed to be wanting, that in company with the other heroes he should, in this time of so great need, give testimony to the truth with his own blood. He gave it in truth, and was among the first to give it, and with such constancy of mind, that, as I was told by one who said he was present at the spectacle and had observed most attentively all that took place, when he put his neck within the murderous halter, he seemed rather to be putting on a regal chain than an instrument of death, such was the alacrity manifested in his countenance. O Blessed man! truly worthy of the fullest confidence of thee, O my country!

On the same day as the priors' execution, with St John's arm already hanging over the monastery gate, a commissioner returned to the London Charterhouse to examine the three monks who now had charge of the community: Bl. Humphrey Middlemore, Bl. William Exmew, St John's confessor, and Bl. Sebastian Newdigate, who was a kinsman of the Earl of Westmoreland and had been a favoured member of Henry VIII's privy chamber. On 25 May, having shown no willingness to reject papal authority, the three were arrested and, for the next two weeks before their trial, they were kept as the picture depicts: chained to pillars by their necks and legs, standing in their own filth. Having been found guilty of treason, they shared their prior's fate on 19 June.

Nearly two years passed until any further martyrdoms but the London Charterhouse was not left in peace: the monks were allowed no books except for the Bible; they were forced to listen to sermons attacking the pope; and a monk from Sheen, who had taken the oath of supremacy, was forced upon them as their prior. On the first anniversary of St John's death, four of the most recalcitrant and influential monks were sent to other houses. Two of them, Bl. John Rochester and Bl. William Walworth, were sent to the Hull Charterhouse; its community had taken the oath. A year later, in 1537, they were on trial for treason because of the contents of a letter sent by Bl. John to the Duke of Norfolk which, it was said, denied the king's ecclesiastical authority and upheld the pope's. Both men were hanged in York on 11 May. Their bodies were not quartered but left to dangle in their chains, rotting.

So by the spring of 1537, the London Charterhouse had experienced prolonged and bloody persecution and many of the community, despite their continued belief in the authority of the papacy, could endure no more. On 18 May sixteen choir monks and twelve lay brothers took the oath. Ten others, however, held out: three priests – Bl. Thomas Johnson, Bl. Richard Beer and Bl. Thomas Green; one deacon – Bl. John Davy; and six lay brothers – Bl. Robert Salt, Bl. William Greenwood, Bl. Thomas Reding, Bl. Thomas Scryven, Bl. Walter Pierson and Bl. William Horn. For eleven days they were left alone but on 29 May they were arrested and sent to Newgate and, as Bl. Humphrey, Bl. William, and Bl. Sebastian before them, they were tied to posts and forced to stand in their own filth. However, since the government did not wish for any more trials, they were left to starve and die in obscurity. By 20 September, except for Bl. William Horn, they had all expired in their chains. That some had lived so long was because of the ministrations of St Thomas More's adopted daughter, Margaret Clement. Having bribed the gaoler, she would enter Newgate disguised as a milkmaid and place food in the Carthusians' mouths and clean up their filth. Bl. William Horn somehow survived starvation and was removed to the Tower, where he remained for three years. In 1540 he was attainted by Parliament for treason and hanged, drawn, and quartered at Tyburn on 4 August. Thomas Cromwell had been executed the week before.

During the restoration of Catholicism under Mary I, the Carthusian martyrs, after More and Fisher, were the most highly-venerated victims of Henry VIII's religious policy. Their sufferings had been recorded by Maurice Chauncy, a member of the London Charterhouse. He had been moved from the house in 1536 at the same time as Bl. John Rochester and Bl. William Walworth, and sent to the Beauvale Charterhouse in Nottinghamshire. He would eventually swear falsely to the Act of Supremacy but by 1547, with other Carthusians, he had fled to the Charterhouse of Val de Grace in Bruges. In 1550, his eyewitness account of the vicissitudes of the London Charterhouse was published and, in 1555, in Rome, a broadsheet of six engravings with an explanatory Latin text appeared telling the story of the Carthusian martyrdoms of 1535 and 1537 in London and York. It was probably intended to mark the end of Juan Alvarez de Toledo's time as the Cardinal Protector of the Carthusian Order, the twentieth anniversary of the martyrdom of St John Houghton and companions, and the re-establishment of the Carthusians in England at Sheen under the priorship of Chauncy.

The broadsheet probably influenced both the message and the style of the wall paintings. The engravings and the text emphasise the martyrs' fortitude and that their sufferings were proof of their constancy to Christ, for such sufferings had been prophesied for his followers in Matthew 23 and 24. Bale had drawn upon the same biblical texts when writing of his Protestant martyrs. The broadsheet also contains no references to miracles; these men had died for the unity of the already established true Church. Its engravings depict the Carthusians in renaissance surroundings and Italianate landscapes with soldiers in Roman costume. Circignani would often do the same throughout the wall paintings at the English College.

A Ob fidem sedi Romanae servatam Ioannes Forestus ordinis S. Francisci de
  observantia sacerdos venerandus vivus suspensus, igneq. subiecto cōbustus
  est, qui accendebatur ligno sacrae Christi statuae.
B Secti sunt in quatuor partes post suspendium spirantes doctor Povvelus,
  Fetherstonus, Abelus sacerdotes docti, Gardinerus quoq. et Larcus Lon-
  dini: Stoneus item Augustinianus Cantuariae.
C Tres R.di Abbates ordinis S. Benedicti necantur, et aliquot ipsorū Monachi la-
          queis suffocantur.

PICTURE XXVII

A. John Forest, an Observant Franciscan and venerable priest, maintains his faith in the Roman See, and is hung alive over a fire which is fed with wood from a holy statue of Christ.

The Observant Franciscans are sons of St Francis who observe strictly, without any dispensations, the Rule of St Francis. They were separated from the Conventuals, who wished to own property, by Leo X in 1517, and declared the true Order of St Francis. By the early 1530s they had seven houses in England, two hundred members and were favoured by King Henry and the royal court. But from the beginning of the king's attacks on the papacy, the Observant Franciscans were his most vocal and united opposition, even willing to preach against anti-papal measures in his presence. So, in the summer of 1534, before the Act of Supremacy had been passed, Henry had all of their houses closed.

Blessed John Forest had been a senior member of the Observants' Greenwich house. It stood close to the royal palace, and Bl. John may have been Queen Katherine's confessor. He suffered early for his opposition to the king's religious policies and, like many of his Order, was sent to prison when his house was closed. Unlike other confrères, however, he survived the ordeal and by early 1538 he was a member of the house of the Conventual Franciscans at Newgate in London. Then, in March or April of that year, he was arrested and, unusually for a Catholic martyr, accused of heresy. The principal charge against him was that he had identified the Catholic Church of the creed with the Church of Rome. He was also accused of saying that St Thomas of Canterbury was a martyr who had suffered for the rights of the Church.

But on 8 May, after some weeks of isolation in his prison cell, Bl. John seems to have wavered and abjured his faith. This was a great coup for the government, and his public recantation at St Paul's Cross was arranged for 12 May. Meanwhile, he was removed from his solitary confinement in prison and allowed to mix with two of his fellow prisoners: the Carmelite Laurence Cooke and the Carthusian Bl. William Horne. Conversation with them seems to have rekindled his faith and stiffened his resolve. When the day arrived for the public recantation, Bl. John refused to go to St Paul's Cross. He was quickly pronounced guilty, therefore, of relapsing into heresy and on 22 May he was brought to Smithfield to be burnt.

A crowd of thousands gathered for the execution, including many notables of the realm, such as Cromwell, Cranmer, the Dukes of Norfolk and Suffolk, the Earls of Sussex and Hertford, and the Bishop, mayor, and sheriff of London. Bishop Latimer preached; Bl. John did not attempt to interrupt him. But when Latimer directly asked whether he would change his mind, the friar responded: 'That if an angel should come down from heaven and show him any other thing than he had believed all his lifetime past he would not believe him, and that if his body should be cut joint after joint or member after member, burnt, hanged or what pain soever might be done to his body, he would never turn from his old sect [profession] of this Bishop of Rome.' And then, referring to Latimer, Bl. John finished by saying, 'Seven years ago he durst not have made such a sermon for his life.'

Circignani accurately shows the friar hanging from a gibbet above the flames. Good states in the accompanying annotation, however, that a statue of Christ was used for firewood. This is not correct. Instead, Cromwell had had the image of Derfel Gadarn or St Derfel the Mighty, a sixth-century soldier, whose equestrian statue was venerated in a somewhat idolatrous manner, brought from its church in Llanderfel for the occasion. The actual wooden horse was left in Wales but the image of St Derfel was set alight beneath Bl. John's feet. 1538 was a year of iconoclasm. Two years before, Cromwell had issued injunctions that were critical of images and relics but in 1538 many shrines, including such places as Walsingham, were despoiled or destroyed. The year culminated with the destruction of St Thomas' shrine at Canterbury and new injunctions which forbade the lighting of candles before images.

B.   Doctor Powell, Fathers Fetherston and Abel, learned priests, and also Gardiner and Larke, are hanged drawn and quartered at London; Fr Stone, an Augustinian, undergoes the same death at Canterbury.

Bl. Edward Powell was born in Wales about the year 1478 and educated at Oxford, where he became a fellow of Oriel College. By 1507 he was also rector of Bleadon in Somerset, and a canon of both Lincoln and Salisbury Cathedrals. After Henry VIII's accession to the throne, Bl. Edward was a favoured preacher at court and his popularity increased during the 1520s because of his writings against Luther. A number of them were well-received and included, for example, a three-part dialogue between himself and the reformer in which he defended the holiness of the pope and the seven sacraments. But he was received rather coldly when he began to defend the royal marriage and became a theological advisor to Queen Katherine. In 1533, Bl. Edward was one of the few English theologians who gave an unfavourable opinion of the king's 'divorce' case. In the same year, he was hired to preach in Bristol against the Protestant sermons of Hugh Latimer, the soon-to-be Bishop of Worcester. In one sermon, Bl. Edward is meant to have condemned secular rulers who 'corrupt and infect the people with open sinning and ill example of living, as he that does put away his first wife and take another without assent or dispensation of the Church.' He returned to Bristol the next year to defend pilgrimages.

On 10 June 1534, Bl. Edward was committed to the Tower of London and lost his benefices for refusing to take the oath of succession. He was attainted of treason at the beginning of November. He was then sent to Dorchester gaol for six months where he was placed in the stocks and denied any bed upon which to lie. Surprising to record, but his subsequent return to the Tower was considered a kindness. He spent the next five years there, refusing to acknowledge the royal supremacy or the validity of Henry's remarriage.

Bl. Richard Fetherston was a graduate of Cambridge and in 1523 was appointed to the archdeaconry of Brecon. From 1525 until at least 1533 he was schoolmaster to Princess Mary and chaplain to Queen Katherine. He was one of the few clerics in the convocation of the province of Canterbury who signed a protest against Henry's proposal to claim the title of Supreme Head on Earth of the Church of England. In December 1534, Bl. Richard was imprisoned in the Tower to encourage him to take the Oath of Supremacy but he persistently refused and was attainted by Parliament for denying the king's supremacy. He was kept locked away, probably in the Tower, until 1540.

Bl. Thomas Abel had been ordained a priest by May 1513 and had become a chaplain to Queen Katherine by 1528. In 1529, he was given a delicate mission. The queen had originally been married to Henry's elder brother, Arthur, Prince of Wales, but he had died only five months after their wedding day and, according to Katherine, had failed to consummate the marriage. Without this ratification of the marriage vows, Henry, despite a biblical prohibition against taking your brother's wife, could marry Katherine. But the king, wishing to be free to marry Anne Boleyn, argued that Arthur had consummated the marriage and so he, Henry, should not have married Katherine. Pope Julius II had issued a bull dispensing Henry and Katherine from the impediment of affinity, in case the marriage had been consummated, and its awkward wording suggested that the marriage may have been consummated. Even though Henry now rejected the worth of such a bull he was citing it as evidence that consummation had occurred. In Spain, however, Emperor Charles V had a brief from 1503 which supplemented the bull and made no reference to any possible consummation, thus undermining the king's argument. Bl. Thomas was given the important task of asking for the brief and bringing it to England. But when he met Charles, he proposed his own and contrary plan: the brief should remain in Spain for safe keeping and the Emperor should urge the pope to move the divorce proceedings to Rome. Charles was convinced by the wisdom of this proposal and did not release the brief. On returning empty-handed, the queen rewarded her chaplain with the rectory of Bradwell-on-Sea, Essex.

Henry then asked the opinion of the University of Paris whether he was right to seek an annulment. The French ambassador informed him that the doctors of the university had voted unanimously in his favour but Bl. Thomas presented the royal council with a list of forty-four Parisian doctors who had dissented. An angry king banished him from court but this did not concern Bl. Thomas. In response to the government-inspired support of Henry's case by Oxford and Cambridge, he published *Invicta veritas*, a work which argued against the king's case, citing texts from the Bible and the Fathers. In 1532, this led to Bl. Thomas' imprisonment in the Tower. He was released the next year but by the end of that year had been re-arrested and remained in the Tower until 1540. In the Beauchamp Tower, you can still see a fine carving by Bl. Thomas in the stone wall of his cell: a bell with the letter 'A' on it, and the name Thomas above.

In July 1540, Bl. Edward, Bl. Richard and Bl. Thomas were attainted of high treason for 'adhering to the bishop of Rome' and denying the king's supremacy. On 30 July they were taken to Smithfield with three Protestants: the *beati* to be hanged, drawn, and quartered for treason; the Protestants to be burnt for heresy. Henry was trying to claim the middle ground between the 'excesses' of Rome and Protestantism. Bl. Edward made the journey tied to Robert Barnes, the Cambridge contemporary and colleague of Bale.

Bl. John Larke served as a priest in the parishes of St Ethelburga's, Bishopsgate, and Woodford in Essex. Then, in 1530, St Thomas More had him appointed as his own parish priest in Chelsea. The Lord Chancellor would serve his Mass and on the day he was summoned to swear the oath to the Act of Succession, St Thomas went to Bl. John for confession and Holy Communion. Bl. Germain Gardiner, a layman, was the nephew and secretary of Stephen Gardiner, Bishop of Winchester. In 1543, he was involved in the 'Prebendaries Plot', an attempt to prove that Thomas Cranmer, Archbishop of Canterbury, was guilty of heresy. It failed. The archbishop kept the trust of the king, who allowed counter-charges of treason against the plotters. Bl. Germain and Bl. John, who, ignorant of any plot, had probably only been arrested because of his connection to More, were found guilty of denying the king's supremacy and on 7 March 1544 they were hanged, drawn, and quartered at Tyburn. They were almost the last Catholic martyrs of Henry VIII's reign.

St John Stone was an Augustinian in Canterbury. We do not know the exact date of his martyrdom but it was probably in December 1539 on the charge of denying the king's supremacy. The city corporation's records of the costs of his execution survive. It is said that in prison, as he waited to die, 'after an uninterrupted fast of three days, he heard a voice, but without seeing the presence of anyone, calling him by name and exhorting him to be of good courage and not to hesitate to suffer with constancy for the truth of the opinion which he had professed.'

C. Three holy abbots of the order of St Benedict are killed. Some of their monks are hanged.

Bl. Richard Whiting was appointed Abbot of Glastonbury, the richest and perhaps oldest monastery in England, by Cardinal Wolsey in 1525. During his time, when many monasteries were declining in numbers, the community of Glastonbury increased from forty-six monks to fifty-four. The whole community took the Oath of Succession in June 1534 and Cromwell, four years later, reassured Bl. Richard against 'fear of suppression or change of life.' The king and his secretary, however, were determined that all religious houses should be found wanting and dissolved. So having discovered incriminating documents, including a book against the king's divorce and a life of St Thomas of Canterbury, the king's commissioners questioned the abbot on 19 September 1539. Bl. Richard was now in his seventies and described as 'being but a very weak man and sickly' but his answers to the questions put to him were considered evidence of 'his cankered and traitorous heart.' At the same time, however, Cromwell rebuked the commissioner who had visited the abbey for giving such a positive report of the abbot. Blessed Richard was sent to the Tower of London and, despite the failure to find any real evidence against him, was sentenced to death at Wells on 14 November. The next day he was dragged on a hurdle to the top of the Tor in Glastonbury and there, beneath the tower of St Michael's chapel, he was hanged, drawn, and quartered, 'at which time,' a contemporary report states, 'he asked God for mercy and the king for his great offences towards his highness . . . and thereupon took his death very patiently.' Two of Bl. Richard's monks died with him: Bl. John Thorne, treasurer of the abbey church, and Bl. Roger James, its sacristan. Their crime was described as sacrilege, in that they had hidden various treasures of the church from the commissioners' grasping hands. At the time of these events, William Good was living in Glastonbury, a boy of twelve years old.

Bl. Hugh Farringdon became abbot of Reading in 1520. During his rule the grammar school attached to the abbey flourished; he supported its work until the last months of his life. Midway between London and Oxford, and not far from Windsor, members of the court often visited the abbey. Blessed Hugh first entertained the king in 1521 when Henry came to make an offering to the abbey's image of 'the Child of Grace'. By 1532 the abbot had become a royal chaplain and in the autumn of 1537 he sang a Requiem Mass for Queen Jane and participated in her burial. Throughout the 1520s, Bl. Hugh had dealt firmly with any of his monks who showed any sympathy to the teaching of Luther. And in April 1533, he was part of a minority at Convocation, who argued that the pope could dispense from the impediment of affinity with a brother's widow, even if the marriage had been consummated. Yet, despite this high understanding of papal authority, he took the Oath of Succession and remained in the king's favour. Nothing, however, could protect his community from Henry's greed and, in August 1539, Bl. Hugh was arrested since it was understood that he would be unwilling to hand over his monastery. He was found guilty of, at least three times, upholding papal authority and on 15 November, the same day as Bl. Richard Whiting, he was hanged before Reading Abbey's gatehouse. Two others were executed with him: Bl. John Eynon, priest of St Giles, Reading, and Bl. John Rugge, a former prebendary of Salisbury Cathedral who had retired to the abbey.

Bl. Thomas Beche was elected Abbot of St Werburgh's Abbey, Chester, in 1527. Having lost this office in 1529 or 1530, he was elected Abbot of St John the Baptist, Colchester, in June 1533. He had signed the petition to the pope in June 1530, appealing for the annulment of the royal marriage, and in 1534 he acknowledged the king's supremacy. In November 1539, however, witnesses were examined at Brentwood, Essex, to incriminate the abbot. It was alleged by them that earlier in the decade Bl. Thomas had said that the pope was the sole supreme head of the Church and that the king had only made the break with Rome to get a divorce. It was also reported that he had described those who had put Fisher and More to death as 'wretched tyrants and bloodsuckers'. What is certain is that a year before, in November 1538, Bl. Thomas had said to the commissioners who had been sent to dissolve Colchester Abbey that, 'the king shall never have my house but against my will and my heart, for I know by my learning that he cannot take it by right and law. Wherefore in my conscience I cannot be content, nor shall he have it with my heart and my will.' The abbot was put on trial for denying the king's supremacy and asserting that all who supported the crown's religious policies were heretics and tyrants. When he had been interrogated beforehand, Bl. Thomas had affirmed the king's ecclesiastical authority and he had pleaded with Henry: 'Be good to me, for the love of God.' At his trial, however, he retracted this statement and, having been found guilty, Bl. Thomas was hanged, drawn, and quartered at Colchester on 1 December 1539.

We cannot imagine how difficult it must have been during this time to remain true to the faith of the Church, when the implications for orthodoxy, if you abandoned the pope, were not yet fully appreciated.

A Propter sedis Romanae et fidei catholicae confessionem, undecim Rᵐⁱ episcopi catholici ex diuturna carceris molestia contabescentes obierunt.

B Phintreus Wodhouse Nelsonus Maijnus, Hansiusque sacerdotes in partes dissecantur.

C Storeus I. V. doctor, Feltonus etiam nobilis, et Shirwodus idem supplicium subeunt, Regina Elizabetha Angliae imperante.

D Quidam vir illustris capite plexus est.

PICTURE XXVIII

A.   Eleven reverend Catholic bishops waste away and perish from the misery of long imprisonment, because they are loyal to the Roman See and the Catholic faith.

Having dedicated three pictures to the Catholic martyrs of Henry VIII's reign, Good now turns to more recent events. Elizabeth I inherited an episcopacy of twenty-one bishops. During her father's time, only one bishop had opposed the king's religious policy: St John Fisher. But by the time of Elizabeth's accession in November 1558, the consequences of disregarding papal authority were understood. The bishops were now willing to defend the fullness of the Catholic faith and suffer for it. Within a year of Mary's death, fourteen of the now seventeen surviving bishops had completely refused the new oath of supremacy. Only one bishop, Anthony Kitchin of Llandaff, having originally refused the oath, would accept the new religious settlement and be restored to his diocese. The version of the oath he was willing to take, however, was a curiously-worded compromise and he refused to participate in the consecration of the new Archbishop of Canterbury. Even the one straying shepherd was fearful of getting lost.

The first member of the episcopal bench to experience the new queen's anger did not survive long enough to refuse the oath. Despite his reputation as a persecutor of heretics, Bishop John Christopherson somehow managed to deliver a sermon from St Paul's Cross ten days after Elizabeth's accession. Standing in the most public pulpit of the realm, he defined Protestantism as 'a new invention of new men and heresies'. He was rewarded for his words by being placed under house arrest and was dead before the end of the year, as were three other bishops.

Queen Mary I's funeral was held on 14 December 1558 at Westminster Abbey. The preacher was Bishop John White of Winchester. Elizabeth had been queen for less than a month but it was evident that she planned to sweep away Catholicism. The bishop, therefore, was extraordinarily brave when he promised certain damnation for all those who 'wilfully departed out of the Catholic Church.' And he praised Mary who 'remembering herself to be a member of Christ's Church, refused to write herself head thereof.' White was immediately placed under house arrest. Early in the New Year he was released but his opposition to religious reform soon landed him in the Tower and on 26 June he was deprived of his bishopric for refusing to take the new Oath of Supremacy, which had come into law the previous month. He died under house arrest on 12 January 1560.

From the beginning of Elizabeth's reign, the bishops fought against royal supremacy in the House of Lords. They were led by Archbishop Nicholas Heath of York, who had been Queen Mary's Chancellor of England. We have already noted his words of opposition during the debate for the proposed Act of Supremacy in the description of Picture II (King Lucius). They were echoed by Bishop Cuthbert Scott of Chester in the same debate. He reminded his fellow peers that the pope was Christ's instrument of unity, Christ's 'vicar general on earth, to govern and rule all his flock.' Furthermore, without the pope, Scott asked 'what certainty can we have of our faith? Or how shall we stay our selves, wavering in the same in this our time?' Peter and his successors were the divine gift of God 'whereunto men might safely cleave and lean, as unto a sure and unmovable rock in matters of faith, knowing certainly that in so doing they shall not fall.' The bishops' united front and passionate arguing failed, however, to prevent the passing of the Acts of Uniformity and Supremacy (though the former was passed by only three votes). Having refused the Oath of Supremacy, Archbishop Heath was briefly imprisoned in the Tower. Yet Elizabeth respected him and, in February 1561, he was allowed to retire to a small estate at Chobham in Surrey. He led a quiet life of recusancy until his death in December 1578. Bishop Scott's refusal of the oath was punished by a heavy fine. When he would not pay, the bishop was committed in May 1560 to the Fleet Prison. He was released on bail two or three years later and confined to a radius of twenty miles from the village of Finchingfield in Essex. He soon escaped to the continent and died in Louvain on 9 October 1564.

Besides White, four other bishops died during 1559. Bishop Ralph Baynes of Coventry and Lichfield, a promoter of the study of Hebrew, was deprived of his see in June 1559 and imprisoned in the London house of Edmund Grindal, the future Anglican Archbishop of Canterbury. He died there on 18 November.

Bishop Cuthbert Tunstall of Durham was eighty-four years old when Elizabeth became queen. He had first become Bishop of London in 1522, had remained loyal to Henry VIII, and, during at least the first few years of Edward VI's reign, had managed to accept Protestant novelties. He refused now, however, to take the Oath of Supremacy and declined to consecrate Matthew Parker as the new Archbishop of Canterbury. He was placed under house arrest and put in Parker's care at Lambeth Palace. He died on 18 November, the same day as Bishop Baynes.

Bishop Henry Morgan of St David's was deprived of his see in the summer of 1559 for refusing to support Elizabeth's religious policies. She allowed him, however, to retire quietly to Wolvercote in Oxfordshire, where he lived with friends until his death on 23 December 1559.

Bishop Owen Oglethorpe of Carlisle upset Elizabeth on her first Christmas Day as queen, when, celebrating Mass in her presence at court, he elevated the Host. She walked out in displeasure. Yet at Elizabeth's coronation, it was the Bishop of Carlisle who placed the crown on her head. He voted, however, against any changes to the religious settlement and died suddenly in London on 31 December 1559 after some months of house arrest. Elizabeth was fortunate with her Catholic bishops: they were quick to die.

On 4 December 1559, five bishops, deprived of their dioceses, made a stand: Heath of York, Bonner of London, Bourne of Bath and Wells, Turberville of Exeter and Pole of Peterborough. They wrote to the queen, warning her against heresy and schism, which she had embraced 'in lieu of the ancient Catholic faith, which hath been long since planted within this realm, by the motherly care of the Church of Rome.' They implored her to copy her sister who, 'being troubled in conscience with what her father and her brother's advisers had caused them to do,' had restored Catholicism and embraced papal authority. Elizabeth was outraged and reminded the bishops of their own schismatic pasts. Who had encouraged her father more than 'you, good Mr Heath, when you were bishop of Rochester? And you, Mr Bonner, when you were archdeacon? And you, Mr Turberville?' She did not understand that the bishops, having tried 'catholicism' without the pope, now accepted that the Church needed him to maintain orthodoxy. Catholicism in England and Wales was in mortal danger but its bishops had matured.

There are seven other bishops whose subsequent lives after their deprivations must be noted: six died under some form of detention; one escaped. Richard Pate had been Bishop of Worcester since 1541, appointed by the Holy See while he was resident in Rome, having fled there because of his opposition to Henry VIII's religious policy. From the pope's point of view, the king had illegally deposed the previous Bishop of Worcester in 1535 and illegally replaced him. At Mary's accession, another crown appointee to Worcester, Nicholas Heath, was transferred to York and, for the first time, Bishop Pate was able to take up residency in his diocese. During his exile, he had been a member of Cardinal Pole's household and he remained close to him in England. Having been deprived of his see in 1559, he was imprisoned in the Tower from 1560 to 1563 and then placed in the care of John Jewel, the Bishop of Salisbury. By strict order, only Protestant servants could approach him, he had to eat alone, he was only provided with Protestant books and he was forbidden to celebrate Mass. In the summer of 1565, he was released from custody on the condition that he remained within London. By the autumn, however, he was probably in Louvain where he may have died on either 5 October or 23 November.

Bishop David Pole of Peterborough may have been imprisoned by the middle of 1561 but he seems to have been released again and, until his death some time between 17 May and 6 July 1568, he seems to have been free of serious constraints. Certainly the Bishop of Lichfield complained that Pole's residence just outside Stafford was unsettling the area because of the visits of 'diverse lewd priests' to him.

During the reign of Mary I, Bishop Edmund Bonner of London was considered to be the fiercest persecutor of heretics, earning him the title 'Bloody Bonner'. He had, however, been an able churchman and conscientious pastor. He was offered the Oath of Supremacy on 30 May 1559. His refusal led to the loss of his diocese and, a year later, to imprisonment in the Marshalsea under the jurisdiction of Bishop Robert Horne of Winchester. He remained there until he died on 5 September 1569. Bonner was taken out once in April 1564 and offered the Oath of Supremacy; to refuse it a second time was a capital offence. When Horne presented the certificate of Bonner's second refusal to the court of queen's bench, Bonner argued that it had no legal force. It named Horne as Bishop of Winchester but under English law, Bonner reminded them,

Horne's consecration was invalid, having been carried out by Matthew Parker whose own consecration as Archbishop of Canterbury in 1559 had not been performed in accordance with the law. Rather than test this argument, the government chose not to proceed with the case.

Bishop Gilbert Bourne of Bath and Wells was sent to the Tower on 18 June 1560. In 1561, he was released into the custody of the Bishop of Lincoln but by the next year he was back in the Tower. During 1563, he was returned to the Bishop of Lincoln, who, by the end of 1565, wished to be relieved of his prisoner. Gilbert eventually died in the custody of the Archdeacon of Exeter at Silverton in Devon on 10 September 1569.

In 1540, Henry VIII created a new diocese out of London: Westminster. It covered most of Middlesex, and Westminster Abbey was its cathedral. Thomas Thirlby was its first and only bishop. In 1550, during the reign of Edward VI, the privy council thought Thirlby too conservative and, wanting to give the bishop designate of London, the reformer Nicholas Ridley, more scope, Westminster diocese was suppressed and Thirlby was transferred to Norwich. Queen Mary then moved him to the more prestigious diocese of Ely. Bishop Thirlby had shown great flexibility so far, willing to work with successive governments and their religious policies but with Elizabeth he held his ground. He voted in Parliament against the Acts of Supremacy and Uniformity and refused the subsequent oath. From 1560 to 1570, Thirlby was either kept in the Tower or at Lambeth Palace as a forced guest of Archbishop Parker. He died on 26 August 1570.

Bishop James Turberville of Exeter was described by a contemporary Protestant as a 'gentleman born . . . very gentle and courteous . . . but most zealous in the Romish religion.' Having refused the oath, he was sent to the Tower on 18 June 1560. He was released in September 1563, after requests by Emperor Ferdinand, and transferred to the custody of the Bishop of London. Two years later the bishop received permission to free Turberville on condition that he remained in the capital and made himself available when required. However, by the end of the year he was back in the Tower where he may have died during 1570.

Bishop Thomas Watson of Lincoln may have been the most able theologian among Mary's bishops; he was certainly one of the finest preachers. Having refused the Oath of Supremacy, and in 1560 having been deprived of his diocese, Watson spent twenty-four years under guard; sometimes in the Tower, at other times as a guest of different bishops. Through the 1570s, as the government became more concerned about Catholic plots, he was held under closer watch, especially after it was discovered in 1577 that he had consecrated the portable Mass set and vestments employed by St Cuthbert Mayne.

Watson's final gaol was specially created for him. Wisbech Castle had been a former palace of the bishops of Ely but its isolated location was unattractive and it had fallen into a state of disrepair. The Bishop of Ely had it repaired and in August 1580, Watson and other Catholic prisoners were moved there. They were not allowed any books, except for the Bible, or any writing materials. In September 1584, after four years in the wilderness of the Fens, Bishop Watson died.

The last surviving bishop from Mary I's reign neither took the Oath of Supremacy nor suffered imprisonment. Bishop Thomas Goldwell of St Asaph was a close colleague of Reginald Pole. He anointed the cardinal the day before he died and witnessed his will. Realising how matters were developing, he fled England in the summer of 1559 and headed for Rome. In 1561, he became guardian of the English Hospice (where he kept rooms until 1578) and arrived in Trent for the final session of the Council. In 1570, he testified in the trial leading to Elizabeth's excommunication and when the students of the new English College in Rome (created from the hospice) rebelled against their first rector, it was Goldwell who recommended to Pope Gregory XIII that the Jesuits take over the institution. He died in Rome on 3 April 1585.

Good refers to eleven bishops suffering imprisonment but of the sixteen surviving bishops in 1559, fourteen suffered some form of confinement. Bishop Pole's situation was very different from Bishop Bonner's or Bishop Watson's, but all had lost their dioceses and were exiles within their own country.

B.   Fathers Plumtree, Woodhouse, Nelson, Mayne and Hanse, are quartered.

Mary, Queen of Scots, fled to England in May 1568. Her presence was a danger to the unmarried and childless Protestant Elizabeth. Mary was the queen's presumptive heir and her Catholicism an attraction to those who opposed the Crown's religious reforms. Plots were quick to develop and, in October 1569, the Duke of Norfolk was sent to the Tower for having planned to marry Mary and place her on the throne.

Other nobles, including Elizabeth's favourite, Leicester, had also been involved.

Then in November, in the north of England, Charles Neville, the Earl of Westmoreland, and Blessed Thomas Percy, the Earl of Northumberland, rose up against Elizabeth. Though disorganised, this northern uprising gained steady support in Lancashire, Yorkshire and Northumberland. Bl. Thomas was motivated principally by religious concerns: English Bibles and copies of the Book of Common Prayer were gathered up and burned, Durham Cathedral was reconsecrated and, on 4 December, Bl. Thomas Plumtree, chief chaplain to the insurgents, celebrated a Latin Mass amidst the cathedral's chevron-striped columns. Less than two weeks later, however, the rising had collapsed and Plumtree was on the run. He was soon captured and condemned to die. On 4 January 1570, he was brought to the marketplace in Durham where a gibbet had been erected. He was offered a pardon if he would apostatise but Plumtree replied that he 'had no desire so to continue living in this world, as meantime to die to God.' He was the first priest to suffer death under Elizabeth; the second was Blessed Thomas Woodhouse.

Bl. Thomas was ordained a priest in 1558, shortly before the death of Queen Mary. The next year he resigned from his parish because of the religious changes. In early 1561, Sir William Cecil, the secretary of state, supposedly discovered a Catholic plot to overthrow the established Church of England. This led to a crackdown during which Bl. Thomas was arrested while celebrating Mass. He was committed to the Fleet prison, where he lived on charity for the next twelve years.

The keeper of the Fleet let Bl. Thomas visit friends in London by day and gave him freedom of the prison. This enabled him to celebrate Mass in his cell, visit the sick and encourage fellow Catholics. In November 1572, Bl. Thomas wrote to Cecil, urging the secretary 'to persuade the Lady Elizabeth (who for her own great disobedience is most justly deposed), to submit herself unto her spiritual Prince and Father, the Pope's Holiness, and, with all humility, to reconcile herself unto him, that she may be the child of salvation.' Cecil was incensed and summoned Bl. Thomas, who infuriated him even more by refusing to recognise his authority because of the queen's deposition by Pope St Pius V two years before. Bl. Thomas was quickly returned to the Fleet and placed in chains. This did not quell his enthusiasm. He wrote short exhortations on obedience to the pope and the true Church, signed them, tied them to stones and threw them out of his cell window. In 1573, the provincial in Paris received Bl. Thomas, by letter, into the Society of Jesus. On 19 June, having been found guilty of refuting the queen's authority, he was executed at Tyburn. As he stood on the scaffold he was ordered to ask pardon of God, the queen and the country. Bl. Thomas replied: 'Nay, on the part of God I demand of you and of the queen that you ask pardon of God and of holy mother Church because, contrary to the truth, you have resisted Christ the Lord, and his vicar upon the earth, the pope.'

Blessed John Nelson, at the age of forty, entered the English College at Douai to study for the priesthood. He was ordained in June 1576 and left for England in November. He worked for a year in London but, while praying the Office, was arrested on 1 December 1577 and imprisoned in Newgate. He was tendered the Oath of Supremacy but refused it because, as he said, 'he had never heard or read that any lay prince could have that pre-eminence.' That was not a capital offence in itself because Bl. John was not of a class obliged to take the oath, but during subsequent questioning, he described the queen as a schismatic and heretic; by an Act of Parliament in 1571, such a statement was high treason and enough to condemn him. On 3 February 1578, Bl. John was dragged on a hurdle from his prison to Tyburn where he was hanged, drawn, and quartered.

Good names Nelson first, but St Cuthbert Mayne was the first seminary priest – trained overseas at the English College in Douai – to be martyred. He was born at Youlston near Barnstaple, Devon, in 1544, and at the age of seventeen, 'not knowing what religion and ministry meant,' became rector of Huntshaw in Devon, through the patronage of an uncle. He went to Oxford, where, in the early 1570s, he came under the influence of Gregory Martin – the future chief translator for the Douai-Rheims Bible – and St Edmund Campion. They were still Protestants but in conversation with them, St Cuthbert became convinced by Catholicism. In 1573, his religious conversion suspected, he was forced to flee and, as Martin and Campion had before him, travelled to Douai. Three year later, St Cuthbert was ordained and returned to England.

He established himself at Golden Manor, the home of Francis Tregian, in Probus, Cornwall. Pretending to be Tregian's steward, St Cuthbert was able to celebrate Mass throughout the county on the extensive family estates and reconcile to the Church those who had faltered. On

8 June 1577, he was sitting in the gardens of Golden Manor when a party of some one hundred men appeared, led by the High Sheriff of Cornwall, Richard Greville. St Cuthbert stole away to his room but, acting on inside information, Greville went straight to the chamber and demanded admittance. On opening the door, St Cuthbert was asked 'What art thou?' to which he replied, 'I am a man.' Unsatisfied by this response, Greville had the priest's doublet ripped open revealing an Agnus Dei case – a wax disc made from an Easter candle, impressed with an image of the paschal lamb and blessed by the pope. It had been outlawed by Parliament in 1571; possession of one meant death. Among St Cuthbert's papers, the sheriff also found a papal bull of Gregory XIII. To bring a papal bull into the country had also been unlawful since 1571 in response to Pius V's bull excommunicating Elizabeth. The punishment for such an offence was again death.

St Cuthbert was paraded through the villages of Cornwall to Launceston Castle and chained up in the dungeons for three months. In the autumn he was tried on a number of accounts, beginning with the possession of a papal bull. The fact that the bull was not concerned with English matters and was out of date, concerned at least one judge, but guilt having been declared, the Privy Council let the conviction stand 'as a terror to papists'. On 29 November, St Cuthbert was examined all day and promised his life if he would swear on the Bible that the queen was the supreme head of the Church in England. He took the Bible, kissed it, made the sign of the cross on it and said, 'The queen neither ever was, nor is, nor ever shall be the head of the Church in England.'

The next day, St Cuthbert was dragged on a hurdle through the streets of Launceston and hanged in the market place. He was allowed to die before his body was cut down and dismembered. When the rector of his seminary, William Allen, heard of the martyrdom, he exclaimed, 'Wretch that I am, how has that novice distanced me! May he be favourable to his old friend and tutor! I shall now boast of these titles more than ever.' Elizabeth's government had successfully winkled out this priest but they were rattled. They had hoped Catholic opposition would die with the aging Marian clergy but the seminary, safe on the continent, promised a continuing tide of young and ardent Catholic priests.

Blessed Everard Hanse was a Protestant minister, who, during a serious illness, grew to doubt his beliefs and was converted to Catholicism by his brother, a Catholic priest. He travelled to Rheims where the English

College, originally founded in Douai, resided from 1578 to 1594. He was ordained in March 1581 and returned to England. Only a few weeks later, he was arrested while visiting Catholic prisoners in the Marshalsea. Admitting immediately that he was a Catholic priest, he was confined in Newgate.

His trial began on 18 July with the prosecution focusing on Bl. Everard's attitude towards papal authority and the validity of the excommunication of Elizabeth. He defended the pope's spiritual authority over England but what condemned him was his confession that he 'would have all men to believe the Catholic faith as I do.' This was enough to find him guilty under a law passed only that year which made it treason to be reconciled or seek to reconcile others to Catholicism. Before he was executed he wrote to his brother. Referring to his own martyrdom, he commented, 'the comforts at the present instant are unspeakable; the dignity too high for a sinner; but God is merciful . . . The day and hour of my birth is at hand, and my master says, "Take up your cross and follow me".' Bl. Everard was hanged, drawn, and quartered at Tyburn on 31 July.

C.   Doctor Storey, a nobleman named Felton, and Sherwood, undergo the same fate at the command of Queen Elizabeth of England.

Having celebrated the earliest martyred priests of Elizabeth's reign, Good now turns to some of the laymen who had laid down their lives for faithfulness to the Catholic Church. On 25 May 1570, a copy of *Regnans in Excelsis*, Pope St Pius V's bull of excommunication and deposition of Elizabeth, appeared nailed to the door of the Bishop of London's palace by St Paul's. This was, in effect, to publish the bull in England and so give it canonical effect. Another copy of it was soon found in the chambers of a well-known Catholic lawyer, who, on the rack, revealed that he had been given it by Blessed John Felton, a man of some wealth. Five hundred halberdiers were quickly surrounding Bl. John's house in Bermondsey and, having been seized, he admitted that he had nailed the bull to the door.

He was imprisoned at Newgate and 'by writing, signed by his own hand,' a contemporary report noted, he treasonably 'declared that the queen . . . ought not to be the queen of England.' He had probably been given the copies of the bull by the chaplain to the Spanish ambassador but he would admit no acquaintance with the ambassador himself. Wanting to know if the queen was in danger, Bl. John became the first Catholic of many to be racked by the authorities for details of feared and imagined plots. He told them nothing; there was probably nothing to tell. On 4 August, at London's Guildhall, Bl. John pleaded guilty to posting the bull and asserting the supremacy of the pope. Four days later he was dragged to St Paul's Churchyard, near the scene of his crime. On the scaffold, pointing to the bishop's door, he declared, 'The supreme pontiff's letters against the pretended queen were by me exhibited there. Now I am ready to die for the Catholic faith.' As his heart was torn out, Bl. John twice uttered Jesus' name.

Bl. John Storey was a brilliant scholar. Around 1541, he became Oxford's first Regius Professor of Civil Law and from 1545 he was an MP. Under Henry VIII, he had taken the Oath of Supremacy but in the first Parliament of Edward VI he opposed the Act of Uniformity and the new Book of Common Prayer, both expressions of a new Protestantism in the land. He particularly incensed fellow MPs by his provocative quotation of Solomon – 'Woe unto thee England when the king is a child' – and found himself in the Tower; the first MP to be sent to prison on the orders of the House of Commons. When he was released he went to Louvain.

Queen Mary's accession brought Bl. John back to England and led to great responsibilities. Besides reappointment to his chair in Oxford he became chancellor of the dioceses of Oxford and London and Dean of the Arches. These were the most important legal positions in the Church. His duties involved him in the persecution of heretics, a work which he embraced and which ensured his murderous reputation among Protestants. In Elizabeth's first Parliament, he defended papal supremacy and was imprisoned in May 1560. Three years later, having escaped once and been recaptured, he escaped again and settled in the Spanish Netherlands.

Desperate for money, Bl. John worked for the Spanish Crown, searching English ships in Antwerp harbour for contraband and heretical books. Some in England wished to make an example of him and one day, in August 1570, he was lured to the quieter port of Bergen op Zoom, ostensibly to inspect an English ship. Once on board, while searching the hold, the hatches were closed and the ship set sail for England. Ten months later he was put on trial in Westminster Hall for planning abroad treasonable acts against the queen. There was no real evidence but the court was genuinely shocked by Bl. John's assertion that he was no longer a subject of Elizabeth having become a subject of Philip II of Spain. He was found guilty of the charge and, on 1 June 1571 at Tyburn, before a vast crowd, including members of the nobility, was hanged, drawn, and quartered.

Blessed Thomas Sherwood was born in London in 1551 to a family who would remain constant in their Catholic beliefs. He travelled to Douai to discuss the possibility of studying for the priesthood at the English College. Having been accepted, he returned home to organise his affairs. He was walking down Chancery Lane in early November 1577, when the cry rang out 'Stop the traitor', and he was arrested. His betrayer was the son of another Catholic family. He quickly admitted that he considered the pope to be the head of the Church. He was brought to the Tower and lodged in a cell which flooded at high tide and, at such times, emitted numerous rats. He was also racked for information about other Catholics and the locations of where he had attended Mass. The only words which he uttered were: 'Lord Jesus, I am not worthy that I should suffer these things for thee, much less am I worthy of those rewards which thou hast promised to give to such as confess thee.' In the New Year, he was found guilty of denying the royal supremacy and, on 7 February, at the age of twenty-seven, Bl. Thomas was hanged, drawn, and quartered at Tyburn.

D.   An illustrious man is beheaded.

The illustrious man is Bl. Thomas Percy, the Earl of Northumberland, who, with Charles Neville, the Earl of Westmoreland, led the northern uprising in November and December 1569, which, as we have already seen, led to the martyrdom of Bl. Thomas Plumtree. Northumberland's father had been executed in 1537 for his role in the Pilgrimage of Grace, a Catholic protest against Henry VIII's religious reforms. The family remained in disgrace after that but were rehabilitated at the accession of Mary. During the early years of Elizabeth's reign they were once more out of favour. This must have made it easier for Bl. Thomas, who had been reconciled to the Catholic Church a year or two before, to write to Pope St Pius V in November 1569 asking him to excommunicate the queen. This elicited a bull of excommunication, *Regnans in excelsis*, in April 1570. Blessed Thomas was prominent in the restoration of the Mass at Durham Cathedral but his heart does not seem to have been in the rebellion itself, for he did little to muster recruits. On 20 December it became clear that the queen's forces were stronger than their own and the two earls fled across the border into Scotland.

Bl. Thomas spent two and a half years in Scotland, mostly as a prisoner. Both Queen Elizabeth and Bl. Thomas' wife offered ransoms for him and, in the end, John Erskine, the regent of Scotland, accepted an offer of £2000 from the English government. Already attainted by

Parliament, Bl. Thomas was not put on trial when he was handed over. Instead, he was brought straight to York and beheaded on 22 August 1572. He may first have been offered a pardon if he would apostatise. It is curious that Good does not name him in the picture. Perhaps, his status as a martyr was doubted, having led a rebellion and died because of it. William Allen, however, after initial doubts, wrote in 1584, 'for, what former quarrel or cause of death soever there was . . . he was offered his life if he would alter his religion.'

Viri plurimi in Anglia pro fide Catholica retinenda hoc qui expressus
est modo consque cruciantur donec universi corporis artus singulatim
luxentur. Sic Edmundus Campianus Societatis Jesu religiosus,
Rodulphus Shernimus, Alexander Briantus, aliique Sacerdotes summi
Pontificis Alumni acerbissime torti fuere. Anno Dñi 1581. 1582. et 1583.

Many men in England, remaining faithful to the Catholic faith, are racked so
severely that their limbs are dislocated. Thus Edmund Campion, a religious of
the Society of Jesus, Ralph Sherwin, Alexander Briant and other priests who have
been students under the Supreme Pontiff, are most cruelly tortured, in the years
1581, 1582 and 1583.

PICTURES XXIX-XXXI

These three pictures depict events that occurred only a year before Circignani began painting. Good devotes so much space to them because the people involved are especially dear to the English College: St Ralph Sherwin, the first martyr of the college; the extraordinary St Edmund Campion; and St Alexander Briant, their companion in death. Good's accompanying annotations, however, remind us that these three priests, though the subject of the paintings, were not the only recent martyrs. Other priests and laymen had laid down their lives for the Catholic faith and, by referring twice to the year 1583 – the year the wall paintings were completed – Good points out to the viewer in Rome that these things – torture and death – are occurring right now. The pictures are not merely a record of the past but a newsreel depicting the present.

St Edmund Campion, born in 1540, was, according to Cecil, 'one of the diamonds of England'. He had a brilliant career at school and then at Oxford, becoming a fellow of St John's. When Queen Elizabeth visited the university in 1566, St Edmund welcomed her on its behalf and the queen's favourite, Robert Dudley, became his patron. The young scholar, however, was increasingly doubtful about the Church of England and found others in Oxford who shared those doubts. He took the Oath of Supremacy and, in 1569, was ordained into Anglican ministry but afterwards he felt 'a remorse of conscience and detestation of mind.' The next year he went to Dublin but in 1571 had to be smuggled out of the country: his Catholic sympathies were increasingly evident and Pope St Pius V's excommunication of Elizabeth in 1570 had made such sympathies treasonable.

Back in England, St Edmund attended Bl. John Storey's trial and then, on his second attempt, he successfully escaped to the English College at Douai, where, after some time, he was ordained a subdeacon. Early in 1573, he went to Rome on foot, perhaps as a penance, in order to join the Society of Jesus and for the next seven years, as he taught, and studied for the priesthood, he lived in Brünn and Prague. There

Qui Summi Pontificis primatum Reginae in Anglia negant tribui posse, tanquam Laesae Majestatis rei damnantur, et ad supplicii locum. Cratibus impositi, ministris interim haereticis ad fidem Catholicam deserendam adhortantibus, per mediam Urbem ignominiose raptantur. Sic Edmundus Campianus cum sociis, aliique Catholici tum Sacerdotes tum laici ad mortem tracti sunt. Anno Domini. 1581 . 1582 . 1583

Those who deny that the primacy of the pope can be given to the queen are condemned for lèse-majesté, and are ignominiously dragged through the city centre to the place of execution on hurdles, while heretical ministers urge them to renounce the Catholic faith. Edmund Campion and his companions, and other Catholics both priests and laypeople, were drawn in this way in the years 1581, 1582 and 1583.

in Bohemia, in late 1579, while teaching philosophy and rhetoric, he received a summons to Rome.

Since the mid-1570s, William Allen, Robert Persons and others had agreed that it was not good enough to train men for the priesthood and then have them wait for Elizabeth's death and, hopefully, a more sympathetic monarch before they would return to England. They believed that England must be converted now, despite the unfavourable political situation. Everard Mercurian, the general of the Jesuits from 1573 to 1580, had serious misgivings about this. He feared that any returning priest, especially after the queen's excommunication, would be viewed by her government as an agent of the pope and a traitor. But his doubts were eventually overcome and he agreed that Jesuits could be part of a new mission as long as their objectives were confined to strengthening the Catholics' faith and reconciling those who, through ignorance or temptation, had been lost. St Edmund was summoned to Rome to be part of this mission.

On 18 April 1580, Robert Persons, St Edmund Campion and others, including St Ralph Sherwin, left Rome for England. News of their mission quickly reached the English authorities, who prepared to arrest them on their arrival. In June, St Edmund wrote to Mercurian that 'something positively like a clamour . . . heralds our approach. Only divine Providence can counteract this kind of publicity.' Could such fears dim St Ralph's excitement? Born in 1549 or 1550, he had proved himself at Oxford a philosopher and a scholar of Hebrew and Greek, and was appointed a fellow of Exeter College. But he left the university to become a Catholic and, in 1577, having studied at the English College in Douai, he was ordained a priest. He then became a member of the English College in Rome. In April 1579, the college oath was administered for the first time. It required that the students promise to return to England when they had completed their studies. St Ralph was the first to take the oath and said that he would go to England, 'Today rather than tomorrow.'

Persons entered England first and, then, St Edmund, disguised as a travelling jewel salesman from Dublin, followed, eventually arriving in London at the end of June, where both Persons and he were sheltered by George Gilbert. St Ralph arrived in August. By then St Edmund had already written his famous 'Brag', It was meant to be an explanation of his motives should he be caught, but the Catholic to whom it was

A. Edmundus Campianus societatis Jesu sub patibulo concionatur, statimque
cum Alexandro Brianto Rhemensis, et Rodulpho Sheruino hujus Collegii
alumno suspenditur.
B. Illis adhuc tepentibus cor et viscera extrahuntur, et in ignem projiciuntur.
C. Eorundem membra ferventi aqua elixantur, tum ad urbis turres et portas
appenduntur, regnante Elizabetha Anno MDLXXXI die prima Decembris.
Horum constanti morte aliquot hominum millia ad Romanam Ecclesiam
conversa sunt.

A.   Edmund Campion of the Society of Jesus speaks to the people on the scaffold.
He is immediately hanged, with Alexander Briant of Rheims, and Ralph Sherwin,
student of this College.
B.   With the breath of life still in them, their heart and entrails are pulled out
and thrown into the fire.
C.   Their limbs are immersed in boiling water, and then hung at the towers and
gates of the city; this all happens on 1 December 1581, in the reign of Queen
Elizabeth. As a result of their constancy in death, some thousands are converted
to the Church of Rome.

entrusted allowed copies of it to be made and it was soon circulating widely among Catholics and Protestants. In it, St Edmund described his mission as 'one of free cost to preach the Gospel, to minister the sacraments, to instruct the simple, to reform sinners, to confute errors; in brief, to cry alarm spiritual against foul vice and proud ignorance, wherewith many of my dear countrymen are abused.'

From August 1580 to Easter 1581, St Edmund travelled around many of the Catholic homes of Berkshire, Oxfordshire, Northamptonshire, Nottinghamshire, Derbyshire, Yorkshire and Lancashire. He wrote to the general of the Society, describing his situation: 'I ride about some piece of the country every day. The harvest is wonderful great . . . I cannot long escape the hands of the heretics . . . I am in apparel to myself very ridiculous; I often change it, and my name also. I read letters sometimes myself that, in the first front, tell news that Campion is taken, which noised in every place where I come so filleth my ears with the sound thereof that fear itself hath taken away all fear.'

St Ralph was taken in November 1580 while preaching in London in the home of a fellow Catholic and alumnus of Exeter College. Imprisoned first in the Marshalsea 'where he lay night and day in a great pair of shackles for the space of a month,' he was then brought to the Tower. On 15 December he was racked for information about his fellow-missionaries and a feared invasion of Ireland. Afterwards, he was left out in the snow. St Ralph was then racked again the next day, and offered a bishopric if he would renounce his faith. He later told his brother that after this he lay five nights and days without any food or speaking to anybody, 'as he thought in a sleep, before our Saviour on the cross. After which time, he came to himself, not finding any distemper in his joints by the extremity of the torture.' He would remain imprisoned for eleven months.

On 27 June 1581 copies of a new work by St Edmund, *Decem Rationes*, were found spread out on the benches of the Oxford University church of St Mary's, where a few hours later students would defend their degree theses. This was an extraordinary publicity coup. The work explained the ten points of the Catholic case which St Edmund would use to refute Protestantism, should a public debate between himself and Protestants be permitted. He concluded with an appeal to Elizabeth that 'the day will surely come that will show thee clearly which of the two have loved thee, the Society of Jesus or the brood of Luther.' The authorities, however, were closing in. On 17 July, through information from a Catholic informer, St Edmund and others were arrested at a Catholic house in Berkshire. He was taken to the Tower and for the next three months interrogated. When questioning failed to solicit the answers the Government wanted, the rack and perhaps other tortures, including metal spikes under his fingernails and the pulling out of his nails, were used. Once, when he was asked how he felt after the previous day's racking, he could only reply, 'Not ill, because not at all.' Four times during August and September he was given, as he had hoped, the opportunity to debate with Protestant divines but while they had warning of the topics and could consult books during the conferences, St Edmund was given no warning and allowed only a Bible (except that at the first conference St Ralph was allowed to assist him).

St Edmund, St Ralph and St Alexander Briant were found guilty of treason in Westminster Hall on 20 November. Their imagined crime was that in Rome and Rheims they had plotted to raise rebellion, invite foreign invasion, kill the queen and change both the government and the established religion. St Edmund led the priests' defence, reminding the jury that 'probabilities, aggravations, invectives, are not the balance wherein justice must be weighed, but witnesses, oaths, and apparent guiltiness.' St Alexander had already suffered much before the trial. A student at Oxford, he had left the university in 1577 to study for the priesthood in Douai. Having been ordained, he returned to England in August 1579 and laboured hard until his capture in March 1581. After six days of starvation he was tortured in the Tower with both metal spikes under his fingernails and on the rack; in fact, his torturer admitted that he was 'racked more than any of the rest.'

In Westminster Hall, after the guilty verdict was read out, the presiding judge asked the priests why they should not be executed. St Edmund replied that while they were prepared to die, their faith was not treasonable and they remained the queen's loyal subjects. Yet the sentence of death was passed. St Edmund's response was to sing the *Te Deum*. He was immediately accompanied by his confrères.

On 1 December 1581, the three priests were dragged to Tyburn. St Edmund was hanged first. He prayed publicly for Elizabeth: 'Your queen and my queen, unto whom I wish a long reign with all prosperity.' A future Catholic martyr, Bl. Thomas Alfield, witnessed his death and later wrote that he was 'an honour to our county, a glass and a mirror, a light and a lantern, a pattern and example to youth, to age, to learned, to unlearned, to religious, and to the laity of all sort, state, and condition of modesty, gravity, eloquence, knowledge, virtue and piety.' The other two priests then had to watch as St Edmund's body was chopped up. Some of the saint's blood fell on a bystander, Henry Walpole, a Cambridge man who was wavering in his faith. That blood changed his life: fourteen years later he himself would be martyred as a Catholic priest.

St Ralph was next. First he prayed for the queen and then said to the crowd that his only crime was being a Catholic. Before being hanged he kissed the hands of the executioner which were covered in the blood of St Edmund. He died with the cry, 'Jesu, Jesu, Jesu, be to me a Jesus!' Two days before in the Tower, he had remarked to St Edmund, pointing to the sun, 'Ah Campion I shall shortly be above yonder fellow.' Having had to watch so much butchery, St Alexander finally met his end. Even as he was about to be hanged he was questioned on the sovereignty of the queen. He kept his composure; he died praying.

A Ob fidem Catholicam in Anglia multi carceres cujusvis conditionis hominibus pleni sunt, in quibus plures fame, paedore, et aliis incommodis oppressi obierunt.

B Varie in catholicos passim animadvertitur. Aliqui ferreis aciculis sub manuum, pedumque unguibus infixis torquentur.

C Alii inaudito quodam tormenti genere, quo corpus variis catenis in unum veluti globum redigitur divexantur.

D Alii pelle ursina induti canibus exponuntur.

E Alii virgis per plateas caeduntur.

F Aliis candenti ferro aduruntur.

G Ad carceres vero Sacerdotes aliquando Sacris vestibus induti, aut aversi equis impositi publice ducuntur.

PICTURE XXXII

A. Many prisons in England, of various kinds, are filled with men who are suffering for the Catholic faith. Many of them waste away and die because of the hunger and filth they suffer.

B. Various forms of suffering are inflicted on Catholics. Some are tormented by sharp needles thrust beneath their fingernails and toenails.

C. Others, undergoing a torment hitherto unheard of, are destroyed by being bound in various chains until their body is compressed into the shape of a ball.

D. Others are dressed in bear skins and exposed to the dogs.

E. Others are beaten through the streets with rods.

F. Others are burnt in the ears with red hot irons.

G. Priests are publicly taken to prison either dressed in their sacred vestments, or facing backwards on horses.

This picture depicts the many ways that both lay people and priests suffered for the Catholic faith. Circignani models it on one of his pictures in San Stefano Rotondo. The public acts of humiliation were designed to demean the individual in the eyes of the spectator. The hidden acts of torture were to extract information and, if there were no real plots to discover, to force a discrediting confession.

Many Catholics, especially lay people, died in prison from deprivation, maltreatment, or disease (A). Having helped a priest, they were locked up and left to rot. When Campion was brought to the Tower he was first placed in the 'Little Ease', where you could neither stand upright nor lie stretched out. The use of needles was originally employed upon suspected witches, whose magic, it was thought, protected them from other types of discomfort (B). Unusually, St Alexander Briant experienced this torture, and St Edmund Campion may have as well.

The 'Scavenger's daughter' was an instrument of torture invented at the Tower during the reign of Henry VIII (C). Circignani probably

never saw one, which explains his inaccurate depiction of it. The English historian, John Lingard, described it like this: 'a broad hoop of iron . . . consisting of two parts, fastened to each other by a hinge. The prisoner was made to kneel on the pavement and to contract himself into as small a compass as he could. Then the executioner, kneeling on his shoulders, and having introduced the hoop under his legs, compressed the victim close together, till he was able to fasten the extremities over the small of his back. The time allotted to this kind of torture was an hour and a half, during which time it commonly happened that from excess of compression the blood started from the nostrils; sometimes, it was believed, from the extremities of the hands and feet.' St Luke Kirby and Bl. Thomas Cottam, who are included in the next picture, suffered this torture.

After he had been arrested, St Edmund Campion was taken to London mounted on a horse (G). He was placed facing the horse's tail, his elbows were pinioned, and his legs were tied under the horse's belly. On his hat a large placard was placed: 'Campion, the seditious Jesuit'. A story had circulated among Catholics in England that a man was dressed in a bearskin and exposed to dogs (D). It did not happen but the imagery connects the sufferings of Elizabethan Catholics with the early martyrs of Rome.

Quod S. Romanae Ecclesiae fidem tenerent, ac praedicarent in Anglia multi Sacerdotes et laici hoc mortis genere occisi sunt anno 1582. 1583. Inter quos hi fuerunt Sacerdotes, Ioannes Shertus, Lucas Kirbeius, et Gulielmus Hartus, huius Ro. Collegii alumni. Robertus, et Laurentius Ionsoni, Gulielmus Filbeius, Kiremannus, Threlkelus, et Hudsonus Collegii Rhemensis alumni. Thomas Cottamus, Ioannes Payuus, Thomas Fordus, Gulielmus Lacius. Complures etiam in singulis Regni provinciis iam condemnati, talem mortem in horas expectant.

PICTURE XXXIII

For holding the faith of the Roman Church and preaching it in England, many priests and laypeople are killed in this way in the years 1582 and 1583. Among them the following are priests: John Shert, Luke Kirby and William Hart, students of this Roman College. Then Robert and Lawrence Johnson, William Filby, Frs Kirkman, Thirkeld and Hudson of the College at Rheims. Then Thomas Cottam, John Payne, Thomas Ford, and William Lacey. Many others are sentenced in the various provinces of the Kingdom, and await execution from one day to the next.

This picture is a pile of bodies, a catalogue of martyrs, which records the most contemporary deaths. In 1583, the year the wall paintings were completed, many of the present students of the college would have known some of these martyrs. They had studied, prayed and lived together. When Circignani had begun painting, some of them had not yet died. And Good makes it clear in his accompanying text that for whatever charges they may have been executed, their only real crime was to be Catholic and preach the Catholic faith. It is hard to imagine what it must have been like for a student to view this picture, where nothing was left to the imagination. Did they place themselves in the top-right corner beneath Tyburn's tree, the three-legged mare?

The first three named martyr priests studied at the English College in Rome. Bl. John Shert was martyred at Tyburn on 28 May 1582. He was found guilty of the same charge as St Edmund Campion and his companions: plotting in Rome and Rheims to kill the queen. As Bl. Thomas Ford was disembowelled in front of him, Bl. John cried out, 'O happy Thomas, happy art thou that thou hast run that happy race! O benedicta anima!' St Luke Kirby had left Rome for England with St Edmund Campion and St Ralph Sherwin but we do not know when he landed in England or when he was captured. He was united with them again at trial and shared their fate at Tyburn, though not until 30 May 1582. Some months before he died, St Luke had written, 'We look to suffer death very shortly, as already it is signified to us. Yet I much fear lest our unworthiness of that excellent perfection and crown of martyrdom should procure me a longer life.' The third Roman martyr is Bl. William Hart, who was executed in York on 15 March 1583. He had been captured the Christmas before in the house of St Margaret Clitherow and was found guilty of receiving assistance from the pope. In his last letter to his mother he wrote, 'Tell me, for God's sake, would you not be glad to see me a bishop, a king or an emperor? Yes, verily, I dare say you would. How glad then may you be to see me a martyr, a saint, a most glorious and bright star in heaven.'

The next six martyrs were students of the first English College, which, originally, had been founded in Douai but from 1578 was in Rheims. Bl. Robert Johnson had been condemned to death with St Edmund Campion. He died at Tyburn with Bl. John Shert on 28 May 1582. Bl. Lawrence Richardson (alias Johnson) was executed at Tyburn two days later with St Luke Kirby. With the rope around his neck, he was offered a royal pardon if he would renounce the pope. Bl. Lawrence replied, 'I thank her Majesty for her mercy; but I must not confess an untruth, or renounce my faith.' Bl. William Filby suffered with him. He had been seized with St Edmund Campion and was only twenty-seven years old at his death. As he stood in the cart beneath the gibbet, one of the sheriff's men asked Bl. William what was in his handkerchief. Finding it to be a little cross of wood, the man held it up to the crowd and cried out, 'Oh, what a villainous traitor is this that hath a cross!' Bl. Richard Kirkman was executed outside York on 22 August 1582. At his trial, when the judge accused him of being a traitor because he was a papist, Bl. Richard replied, 'You might, sir, with the same justice, charge the Apostles also with being traitors, for they taught the same doctrine that I now teach, and did the same things for which you condemn me.'

Bl. Richard Thirkeld was already an old man when he was ordained a priest in 1579. He was captured in March 1583 in York and found guilty of reconciling subjects of the queen to the Catholic Church. When the usual barbarous sentence was passed, Bl. Richard fell to his knees and exclaimed, 'This is the day which the Lord hath made: let us be glad and rejoice therein.' He was executed outside York on 29 May. His death is the most recent martyrdom to be recorded in the wall paintings. We have covered a lot of ground since the first century and the 'visits' of St Peter, St Joseph of Arimathea and St Simon. The last named Rheims martyr is Bl. James Thompson (alias Hudson), who was hanged on 28 November 1582. Just before he was turned off the ladder, he interrupted his prayers and turned his head a little towards the spectators and said, 'I had forgotten one thing. I pray and beseech you all to bear witness that here I die in the Catholic faith.'

The picture's inscription concludes with the names of four other recent martyrs. Good did not include the first, Bl. Thomas Cottam, with the martyrs from the English College in Rome, but today Bl. Thomas is classed as a former student of the college. Bl. Thomas was executed at Tyburn on 30 May 1582 with Bl. William Filby, Bl. Lawrence Richardson and St Luke Kirby. He was the last to die, having first watched the dismemberment of his three companions. St John Payne was a Douai man who worked principally in Essex with the support of the Petre family of Ingatestone Hall. He was executed in Chelmsford on 2 April 1582. Known in the county to be a good man, the bystanders asked that he be allowed to hang until dead. Bl. Thomas Ford was seized with St Edmund Campion and was executed at Tyburn with Bl. John Shert and Bl. Robert Johnson on 28 May 1582. Finally, Bl. William Lacey was captured on 22 July 1582 in York Castle, having just sung a High Mass for the Catholic prisoners. He was hanged, drawn, and quartered a month later on 22 August with Bl. Richard Kirkman.

The last sentence of Good's inscription reads, 'Many others are sentenced in the various provinces of the Kingdom, and await execution from one day to the next.' This forcibly reminded visitors to the College that this picture was not just describing past sufferings, however recent, but also present persecutions.

A | Gregorius XIII. Pont. Max. huius Anglorum Collegii fundator, ac parens
optimus Alumnos suos Christo commendat: ut, quos in Angliam ad fidei
defensionem mittit, adversus hostium insidias, atq. tormenta, divina virtute
confirmet: qua freti iam aliquot pro Catholica Romana ecclesia
fortiter occubuerunt.

B | Philippus Boncompagnus S.R.E. presb. Card. tit. S. Sixti eiusdem
Pont. Fr. Fil. Collegii Protector, et Benefactor munificentiss. idq. a Deo precatur.

Picture XXXIV

A. Pope Gregory XIII, founder of this English College, and a true father, commends his students to Christ. He prays that Christ may strengthen with divine power, against all the snares of the enemy, those whom the pope sends to England to defend the Catholic faith. Relying on this divine power, some have already bravely given their lives for the Church, Roman and Catholic.

B. Filippo Buoncompagni, Cardinal of the Holy Roman Church with the title of St Sixtus, and the nephew of Pope Gregory, protector and most generous benefactor of the College, makes this prayer his own.

This is a family photograph: the English College staff and students of 1583, some faces probably painted from life, pray with Pope Gregory XIII, their founder and benefactor. Movingly, Gregory looks to the cross while gesturing towards the students; he is interceding for them, caring for them, as the popes have cared for England and Wales since, according to Good, even the days of St Peter. They are joined by the pope's nephew, Cardinal Filippo Buoncompagni, who, as the college's cardinal protector from the end of 1580 to mid-1586, had special care for the seminary. What exactly are they (including the student with the rosary beads, which in England were now illegal) praying for? Good tells us that they are praying for Christ's power so that they may defend the Catholic faith in England. Any tentativeness, therefore, has passed. The pope, the cardinal protector and the students are committed to the mission and, unmistakably, at the end of these thirty-four pictures, they are committed to martyrdom. Fired by the example of fellow students and moved by recent discoveries of Rome's own early martyrs, the students view these depictions, not to be warned of the reality of martyrdom, but to be inspired by its glory. And these pictures have ensured that the English and Welsh Catholic martyrs are still celebrated.

In 1886, a decree of the Congregation of Sacred Rites declared that fifty-four martyrs of the reigns of Henry VIII and Elizabeth I were *beati*, for the following reason:

> After Gregory XIII had caused the sufferings of the Christian martyrs to be painted in fresco by Nicholas Circignani, in the church of St Stephen on the Caelian Hill, he permitted also the martyrs of the Church in England, both of ancient and of more recent times, to be represented in like manner by the same artist in the English church of the Most Holy Trinity in Rome, including those who from the year 1535 to 1583 had died under King Henry VIII and Queen Elizabeth, for the Catholic faith, and for the primacy of the Roman Pontiff. The representations of these martyrdoms, painted in the said church, remained, with the knowledge and approbation of the Roman Pontiffs who succeeded Gregory XIII for two centuries, until they were destroyed by wicked men about the end of the last century.
>
> But copies of them still remain; for in the year 1584, with the privileges of the said Gregory XIII, they had been engraved at Rome on copper-plate, with the title: *Sufferings of the Holy Martyrs, who for Christ's sake and for professing the truth of the Catholic faith, have suffered death in England both in ancient and more recent times.*

The engravings of these wall paintings proved, therefore, that Gregory XIII had acknowledged the executed men depicted to be martyrs and had permitted them to be venerated as such.

St Thomas More had spent his time in the Tower meditating upon the Passion of Christ. This divine example of suffering gave him the strength to endure his own sufferings and face death. In this picture, Pope Gregory XIII looks towards the cross, seeking that same strength for the students. Christ is the King of Martyrs; only his strength is sufficient. St Edmund Campion could have been thinking of this scene when he wrote, at the end of his 'Brag', the following words:

> Many innocent hands are lifted up for you daily and hourly by those English students whose posterity shall never die, which beyond seas, gathering virtue and sufficient knowledge for the purpose, are determined never to give you over, but either to win you heaven or to die upon your pikes.

Conclusion

Our first chapter began where John Bale was born, in the tiny Suffolk village of Covehithe. The parish church, dedicated to St Andrew, must have been magnificent, built over time in both the Perpendicular and Decorated Gothic styles. Except for the tower, all is now in ruins. Some external walls remain but their windows are large, gaping holes, bereft of glass and tracery. Within the shell of the church, crouching against the tower, is a squat thatched building put up after the Civil War. This replacement House of God is a simple affair, green, in patches, with damp. Is this Bale's legacy to his home: a magnificent Catholic church, a jewel, replaced by a whitewashed cottage? Bale had declared war upon the saints of England and Wales. He connived at their destruction: images were painted over, stained glass was smashed and statues were burnt. England and Wales' history was altered; their former saints and heroes were trashed.

Yet a thousand miles away, south of the Alps, the history of England and Wales was preserved and cherished; what Bale buried, the English College resurrected. Painted apostles, kings, priests, martyrs and missionaries form a procession around the church walls, teaching us our past, encouraging us for the future. They speak of a forgotten calendar of saints, of a plundered landscape of shrines. The wall paintings of the English College echo the words of St Edmund Campion, spoken to the judge and jury after he had been sentenced to death:

> In condemning us you condemn all your own ancestors – all the ancient priests, bishops and kings – all that was once the glory of England, the island of the saints, and the most devoted child of St Peter. For what have we taught, however you may qualify it with the odious name of treason, that they did not uniformly teach?

Bibliography

In an attempt to make this book more inviting, I have refrained from using footnotes, but here are some books which would allow you to pursue much more deeply certain parts of this study.

General

I am completely indebted to, and have followed closely, Anne Dillon's magnificent work: *The Construction of Martyrdom in the English Catholic Community, 1535-1603*. Ashgate, 2002.

The English College

Williams, Michael E, *The Venerable English College*. Gracewing, 2008.

John Bale

Fairfield, Leslie P, *John Bale*. Wipf & Stock, 2006.

Thomas More

Ackroyd, Peter, *The Life of Thomas More*. Chatto & Windus, 1998.

Cardinal Reginald Pole

Duffy, Eamon, *Fires of Faith – Catholic England under Mary Tudor*. Yale, 2009.

Jerome Nadal

Nadal's annotated illustrations of Gospel stories can be viewed at this website: http://catholicbibleresources.net/Art/Nadal.htm

British saints

Farmer, David, *Oxford Dictionary of Saints*. OUP, 2003.
Thurston, Herbert J and Attwater, Donald eds, *Butler's Lives of the Saints*. Christian Classics, 1990.
Stanton, Richard, *A Menology of England and Wales*. Burns and Oates, 1892.